The All-Time World Cup

THE QUEST FOR FOOTBALL'S GREATEST TEAM

David Brooks

The Parrs Wood Press
Manchester

First Published 2002

THE PARRS WOOD PRESS
St Wilfrid's Enterprise Centre
Royce Road, Manchester, M15 5BJ
www.parrswoodpress.com

© **David Brooks 2002**

ISBN: 1 903158 29 X

	Suffolk County Council
	Libraries & Heritage
CYPHER GROUP	24.6.02

Photographs courtesy of Empics

This book was produced by The Parrs Wood Press and Printed in Great Britain by:

Fretwell Print & Design
Healey Works
Goulbourne Street
Keighley
West Yorks BD21 1PZ

CONTENTS

PHOTOGRAPH SECTION BETWEEN PAGES 96 AND 97

To all those who put up with my rambling,
And to Deb, who made me believe.

ACKNOWLEDGEMENTS

As with any project that extends over several years, there have been a great number of people who've had some sort of input at one time or another. An idea here and an opinion there, you've all played an important part, so thank you.

Special thanks to Ruud Doevendans, the Dutch maestro, whose knowledge of international football continues to astound, and to Alex Trickett, my most valuable sounding-board.

Others who've helped fill in gaps include members of the RSSSF: Gerhard Öhlinger, Misha Miladinovich, Jose Luis Pierrend and Luis Fernando Passo Alpuin, as well as Alex Gotnik and Julio Marcías. The RSSSF's vast array of statistical information was also of great use.

A mention also to Mum, Dad, Deb and Paul, who lent me their eyes and to Kate for opening doors.

The help of Alistair Brown, who designed the cover, was invaluable, and thanks also to Lynn Trickett for her support.

Finally, a big thank you to Andy Searle of The Parrs Wood Press, who gave me the chance to make an idea a reality.

INTRODUCTION

Selecting "All-Time England sides" has become something of a national pastime in recent years. Newspapers, magazines, video-makers and armchair pundits are all at it. Perhaps it's England's disappointing World Cup performances that make us dream? Surely the World Cup would be England's for the taking if only they could bring back Charlton and Moore, or if Matthews was able to supply the crosses for Lineker and Greaves? It's a tempting thought, but then it's not as simple as that. Forget the fact that it's all a fantasy anyway, and think about what England's opposition would be if every country were able to pick a selection of their greatest-ever players. Suddenly, England would have some serious competition.

Over the last ten years I have meticulously researched the football histories of over 25 countries, keen to rid myself of an Anglo-only perspective that traditionally haunts selections of "The Greatest Players", and "All-Time XIs".

This book is the result of those endeavours. In the following pages you'll find team selections for 16 football powers, and an evaluation of their relative strengths. The assessment is made by way of a World Cup-style tournament, culminating in the ultimate match - "The All-Time World Cup Final".

Of course, at the end of the day, it's merely one man's view on the world. Hopefully, it's an educated view, forged from reading, watching and talking about as much football as possible, but it's still just opinion which will doubtless lead to more debates.

Fortunately, the sports media has been a huge help. At regular intervals, newspapers and football publications have printed lists of the top players to grace the game. The trick is separating the wheat from the chaff. Some people know what they're talking about, others plainly do not. One such poll resulted in Teddy Sherringham being crowned one of the top 100 players ever. Now Teddy's a good player, but come on...

Qualifying and seeding

The first task was to pick the 16 teams that would contest the finals. It was suggested that the selection should be based strictly on past success in the World Cup, and certainly that would have simplified matters. But it would also miss the point. The purpose of this book is not to discover which countries have been most successful in the World Cup. A quick look at the history books will tell you that. Brazil have won four World Cups, Germany and Italy three each - case closed. But that doesn't necessarily mean they would have the best all-time teams. It's possible for a country to have produced a plethora of quality players without ever having succeeded in a single World Cup. If a county unearths a couple of stars each decade, then their All-Time team will look pretty good. Consequently the teams examined in these pages are those with the best player resources at their disposal. Of course, there are many teams that are closely matched, and any of ten to fifteen teams could have taken the last five or six spots in the tournament. The ones selected hopefully represent a good balance of styles and eras, and, with the qualification of Scotland and Ireland, should fuel home interest

Of the finalists, seven have won the World Cup. These teams were automatically seeded, along with Holland - the next most successful of our finalists. No more than two seeds were allowed in each group and the remaining teams were placed at random.

A balanced approach

All too often, elite team selections are loaded with attacking players. Ball dribblers and goal scorers naturally attract attention and affection, but no team can be successful without balancing ball players with ball winners, and this book is about finding the best *team*. Of course, different countries have different styles and I've tried to reflect those traditions in the team selections and formations.

Most of the line-ups feature four at the back and at least one ball winner. Over the last century various different tactics emerged. In general, teams have become more defensive over time, so that from the days of the "Pyramid formation" and "Motedo", when two defenders was the norm, we now regularly see teams with five at the back.

In general I've used relatively modern tactics, although it's worth noting that as far back as 1950, Uruguay were effectively playing 4-3-3. No team has won the World Cup with less than four defenders since 1954.

Most of the team selections feature more than one midfield playmaker. Many of the best players have filled that role, so there's a natural logjam to sort out. I've taken the stance that a team can usually accommodate two or three such players, even if one ultimately emerges as the team's focal point. There's some precedent here. In 1970 Mário Zagallo selected a forward line for Brazil that included five inside lefts. Pelé, Gérson, Rivelino and Tostao were all generals in some sense, but Zagallo obviously made do because Brazil won the World Cup at a canter.

INTRODUCTION

Eligibility

A player doesn't have to have represented his country to be eligible for this competition, although in actuality no uncapped player made the grade. Several were capped by more than one country, taking advantage of more lenient eligibility standards. Today it sounds strange to think that a player could represent one country and then go and play for another, but until the 1960s it was fairly common.

Rules now state that once you've played a full international for one country, you can't play for another. I've retroactively applied the rule, so whichever country a player first represented will be their team for this tournament. Tough on Spain and Italy, but then it wasn't exactly fair on Argentina and Uruguay when the European nations poached their stars in the 1930s and 1950s.

Coaches

For each team I selected a coach. You'll see phrases like "the coach decided it was time for a change". Of course the coach didn't really make the decision, but hopefully it adds something to the fantasy.

A question of location

Every party needs a venue, but the All-Time World Cup will have to be the exception. Choosing one of the established football powers to host the competition would give that country an advantage - England at Wembley or Brazil in the Maracana would be tough to beat. On the other hand, choosing a neutral venue, like the USA, seems pointless. Let's just say that every game is played in that super-stadium in the sky that favours neither team, while generating its share of enthusiastic support.

A dose of reality

This isn't really intended as a reference book but you'll find plenty of recollections of football history. Every effort has been made to ensure factual accuracy, but doubtless, there are mistakes.

Throughout these pages you'll find player profiles and reports from important real-life World Cup matches, interspersed with the fictional games and team profiles. These are intended to provide some additional information

9

and perspective, substantiating team selections and match results. The real-life matches were selected on the basis of their relevance to this competition. For example, the German and Dutch line-ups both include multiple players from the teams that fought out the 1974 World Cup Final. That Munich clash might therefore give us some clues as to what would happen in an "All-Time" fixture.

Head-to-Head

In the knock-out stages you'll find a Head-to-Head feature, which aims to provide an indication of the two teams' relative strengths. It's not a perfect science but what the hell?

That's about it. Hope you enjoy it, and remember, it's all about opinions.

David Brooks
Atlanta and Warrington, 2002

THE CONTENDERS

The footballing pedigrees and histories of the finalists in the All-Time World Cup varied enormously, but each had one thing in common - a battery of quality players.

Brazil started as favourites, as they usually do. No team makes the game seem quite so effortless, quite so - well yes, beautiful - as the boys in gold and blue. This particular selection of footballing artists was especially pleasing. Starting with the incomparable Pelé, and continuing with Garrincha, Zico, Didi and Gérson, it was hard to see how so much talent could be harnessed in one unit. If coach Zagallo could find a way, the possibilities would be breathtaking.

The Italians were also contenders, although their main strengths were altogether different. If defence really wins championships, then this was the time to prove it. In Baresi, Maldini and Facchetti, the Azzuri boasted some of the finest defenders ever, but even they had never seen attacks quite like these before.

One of the most potent forward lines belonged to Argentina. For so long the victim of European poaching, they now had a full compliment of resources to pick from. The team would be bolstered by the recall from Italy of the mighty Luis Monti in midfield and Raimundo Orsi, who'd be available on the wing. There were great defenders too, but it was in attack that the Argentines looked most devastating. Maradona, Di Stéfano, Batistuta, Moreno and Kempes hoped for starting places, the opposition just hoped to stay out of their path.

If there was one team that relied on great players less than the others it was Germany. No unit would be as organised, as disciplined and as strong-willed as the Germans, a testament to their unfailingly solid World Cup performances of the past. Unfortunately for the other contenders, this time Germany had a brilliant system and magnificent players. Müller, Matthäus, Rummenigge, the imperious Beckenbauer - just frightening.

England, of course, brought its own greats to the party. Matthews, Charlton, Moore and Banks could stand comparison with anyone, and now they would need to prove their legendary worth. Despite only having won the World Cup once, no one could match England's length of history. Their ability to field players who had starred in eight or nine different decades gave the country that founded the game guile, experience, and at least half a chance.

Many felt the Dutch had an even better shot. Certainly the greatest footballing nation never to have lifted the World Cup, Holland now had their chance to right a few wrongs. Cruyff, Neeskens, and Krol from the Total

11

Football side of the 1970s joined Gullit, Van Basten, Rijkaard and Koeman, who had starred some ten years later. Throw in Bergkamp and Davids and the makings of a champion seemed to be there. Then again, the Dutch often had enough talent. This time, in this company, they'd have to harness it to maximum effect.

The French were the only other realistic winners, and with the emphasis on the modern, power, as well as poise, was the order of the day. Desailly, a one-man wall at the back, and Fontaine, the most prolific marksman in a single World Cup, served as useful bookends, but it was the midfield that made the best reading. Platini, Zidane, Kopa and Tigana - 90 minutes wouldn't be long enough.

Of the teams in the next tier, Uruguay were the hungriest. Twice winners of the Cup - but not for half a century - the Uruguayans were intent on regaining some pride. Andrade, Varela and Nasazzi, none of whom had ever lost a World Cup match, would be there to see the job got done.

The unseeded countries were unlikely to win, but such was the quality brimming in every squad, that any of them could upset a favourite on a given day. Think Hungary's Puskas or Austria's Ockwirck would be intimidated by a Beckenbauer or Pelé? Not a chance. If Italy had Piola and England had Banks, then Portugal had Eusébio and Russia had Yashin. For every Koeman, there'd be a Gustavsson, for every Meazza, a Suárez or a Sindelar. There wasn't a team in the tournament without at least a couple of all-time greats and as such each team had a fighting chance.

The biggest outsiders were Scotland and the Republic of Ireland. Some were surprised that the tartan ones made it this far, but the team sheet tells the story. Law and Dalglish formed potentially one of the best strike forces in the competition, and, for once, depth would not be a problem. A history stretching back to the first ever international gave the Scots plenty to chose from, and besides, qualifying for tournaments had never been the hard part. Staying there wouldn't be any easier this time.

Ireland's task was perhaps even more difficult. They'd qualified by defending stoutly against more gifted opponents and relied heavily on stars from big English clubs. In fact, all 10 of the outfield starters, which included the likes of Roy Keane and Liam Brady, had experience with Manchester United, Liverpool or Arsenal, which sounds impressive, but would probably count for little at this level.

The quality of the field was illustrated by the number of excellent teams - and great players - that failed to get beyond the qualification phase. A Yugoslavian (Serbia and Montenegro) team containing Sekularac and Dzajic had missed out, as had Croatia, who boasted Katalinski, Zebec, Boban and

Suker, but still didn't have enough. Neutral observers could only lament the loss and wonder what might have happened had the two sides competed as one (as they have for most of their footballing history). The Czechs and Slovaks suffered a similar fate. Together, they'd twice finished runners-up in the World Cup, apart they didn't even make the finals, which would miss the likes of Masopust, Plánicka and Nejedly. Although the break up of the Soviet Union had a similar - diluting - effect, the Russians had survived. Ukraine had not, despite the efforts of Blokhin, Kuznetsov and Shevchenko, while a strong defence had not been enough for Georgia.

Other high profile casualties included Belgium with Van Himst and Scifo, Denmark, who had the Laudrup brothers, Simonson and Schmeichel, and Poland, who added Boniek and Pol to a team based around the great side of the 1970s, including Deyna and Lato.

While England and Scotland had progressed, the other Home Nations had faltered, which meant no stage for George Best, who vies with Di Stéfano for the title of greatest player never to participate in the World Cup finals. A Welsh side containing Charles, Rush, Giggs and Meredith had put up a good fight but lacked punch in midfield.

Chile, Bulgaria, Peru, Cameroon; Figueroa, Stoichkov, Cubillas, Milla. The list of those lost before the finals began made uncomfortable reading, but the cast of stars that would be on show promised full compensation.

BRAZIL

Beautiful flair

Mário Zagallo's selection as coach was a little controversial - many preferred Vicente Feola, who'd had the foresight to introduce Pelé and Garrincha in 1958 - but the nature of this particular task called for Zagallo's special skills. No coach has ever succeeded in incorporating as many talented players (many of whom played the same position) as with Zagallo's Brazil in 1970. Selecting the All-Time team would require similar levels of diplomacy and imagination.

Forwards

Brazil's choice of attacking players was simply incredible, but such depth created as many problems for the coach as it would for the competition. Pelé was a sure thing, of course, as was Garrincha, but after that it got tricky. Would Rivelino or Zagallo himself play on the left? Would it be Didi or Gérson in the playmaker role? Where would Zico fit in, not to mention Rivaldo? And who should partner Pelé? Tostao had done the job better than anyone else, but Ademir, Leônidas, Ronaldo and the slick Romario were all champing at the bit. Zagallo eventually decided that Pelé, the all-round attacking genius, would be assisted by Romario, the sharp, arrogant goal scorer. Zico would have to come off the bench - a travesty in the eyes of some, but the White Pelé had rarely shone at the World Cup, with the enchanting exception of 1982.

Midfielders

Zagallo tried to pick complimentary talents in his 4-4-2 formation, which would switch to 4-3-3, and even 4-2-4 when circumstances allowed. So to balance the brilliance of Garrincha on one wing, the composure and style of Rivelino on the other.

Didi got the start in the middle, frankly because he, and not Pele, had been the key player in the 1958 side, which stands as perhaps Brazil's greatest. Rivaldo might get a few cameo performances, but his body of work isn't yet complete (same story with Ronaldo), and Brazil had no need for unfinished products.

Further back, Brazil's talent pool was less formidable. Cerezo, Zito and Dunga would fight for the holding role. Cerezo, an unheralded hero of that remarkable 1982 side, would get the first shot.

Defenders

The starting central defenders would be the 1986 pairing of Júlio César and Edinho. The best combination in Mexico, they would be more severely tested this time.

If Brazil were strong in one area of defence, it was at full-back, possibly because their flank defenders weren't really defenders at all. Carlos Alberto and Cafu on the right, Roberto Carlos and Júnior on the left - all exuded attacking flair usually reserved for the great wingers. There were more conventional defenders as well. Jorginho from the early 1990s and the two Santoses - Djalma, the goliath on the right, and Nílton, the smooth veteran on the left. Zagallo plumped for Alberto and Nílton Santos, a combination that most rated as the best in the competition.

Goalkeepers

Brazil have fielded some average goalkeepers in their time (Felix, Carlos, even Emerson Leão) but for this tournament only one gem was required. In Gilmar, of 1958 and 1962 fame, Brazil had that one respectable goalkeeping presence. Taffarel, Brazil's most capped player, would serve as a decent enough reserve.

14

In all, the Brazilian side looked frightening. It boasted five players from the 1958 side, three from 1970 (Pelé is included in both counts), three players from the 1980s, and Romario from the 1994 unit.

Not a bad spread, but a bit harsh on Leônidas, who helped start it all back in 1938. Indeed, had he played against Italy in the semi-finals, perhaps he and not Pelé, would have been the national hero. The obscenely skilled Ademir could tell a similar story. A World Cup loser only because Uruguay chose the day of the deciding match of the 1950 World Cup to play their single greatest game.

With giants such as those and Jairzinho on the bench, it was only natural that Brazil started favourites.

Starting line-up (4-2-4)
Gilmar; Carlos Alberto, Júlio César, Edinho, Nílton Santos; Cerezo, Didi; Garrincha, Romario, Pelé, Roberto Rivelino

BRAZIL WORLD CUP RECORD

Year	Result	P	W	D	L
1930	Eliminated in round one	2	1	0	1
1934	Eliminated round one	1	0	0	1
1938	Eliminated in semi-finals (3rd)	5	3	1	1
1950	Lost in Final	6	4	1	1
1954	Eliminated in quarter-finals	3	1	1	1
1958	Winners	6	5	1	0
1962	Winners	6	5	1	0
1966	Eliminated in round one	3	1	0	2
1970	Winners	6	6	0	0
1974	Eliminated in round two (4th)	7	3	2	2
1978	Eliminated in round two (3rd)	7	4	3	0
1982	Eliminated in round two	5	4	0	1
1986	Eliminated in quarter-finals	5	4	1*	0
1990	Eliminated in round two	4	3	0	1
1994	Winners	7	5	2**	0
1998	Lost in Final	7	4	1**	2
Totals		**80**	**53**	**14**	**13**

*Lost one game on penalties
**Won one game on penalties

ENGLAND

One trophy, many great players

The choice of England coach was straightforward. Alf Ramsey won the World Cup. No-one else did - end of debate.

Team selection was more difficult. Gordon Banks or Peter Shilton; Jimmy Greaves or Gary Lineker; Bryan Robson or Duncan Edwards. There were some close calls for Ramsey to make in choosing his All-Time team.

Forwards

Up front, England were faced with a number of questions. Greaves, a legend as much for his style as his 43 goals in 56 internationals, was the fans' favourite, but just one goal in seven World Cup matches raised some questions about his record against the very best defenders. With the standard of opposition about to be raised another notch, one could understand why Ramsey, who'd famously left Greavsie out in 1966, might be tempted to do so again.

Lineker, on the other hand, had never struggled to adapt to the international stage. England's greatest goal scorer - even if Bobby Charlton owns the goal scoring record - the only real question was who should partner him. If not Greaves, then maybe Kevin Keegan, twice European Footballer of the Year, or Tommy Lawton, who starred both pre and post-war. Alan Shearer and Michael Owen were also mentioned, so the options were plentiful. At one point Shearer looked destined to set himself apart as England's greatest goal scorer, but his career lost momentum after Euro 96. Owen's form - and selection as European Footballer of the Year - in the build up to Japan/Korea 2002 was good enough to suggest that he might one day be an All-Time first choice, but he'd hover on the bench for this tournament.

Midfielders

If there was a nagging feeling that none of the strikers would be quite good enough at the All-Time level, there were no such worries about the midfield. Bobby Charlton has easily the greatest international reputation of any England player, and one that is well deserved. Tremendous shooting power, 49 goals, a World Cup winner; the list goes on. The only debate was where to play him. Although his most famous performances came in the middle, the most vivid memories are of him on the left wing where he starred during the World Cup of 1962 in Chile. Playing him wide, however, would mean re-igniting the old Tom Finney-Stanley Matthews debate. Outside the UK there is no debate. Matthews is considered one of the finest right-wings ever (only Garrincha is consistently ranked above Sir Stan), while Finney never really made an impact in three World Cups. His reputation at home would ensure he'd challenge for a place, even if his selection over Matthews was no longer an option. Cliff Bastin would act as wing cover.

If Charlton played inside, then Ramsey had to choose between two power house Manchester United players in the middle. Duncan Edwards, the biggest talent lost in the Munich crash, could play anywhere, but he seemed best suited to the holding role that Bryan Robson also coveted. The talismanic Edwards proved irresistible to Ramsey, but Robson's 26 goals in 90 internationals made a compelling case.

Two modern idols, Paul Gascoigne and David Beckham, would look to force their way in as the competition progressed. Gascoigne is arguably the most talented English footballer of the last 30 years, while Beckham's combination of skill and incredible work rate made him a difficult omission.

Defenders

The defence looked solid, if unspectacular. Three of the back four (flat, of course) had played together in Chile, 1962, where Jimmy Armfield had looked the best right-back, and Ray Wilson had found Garrincha too hot to handle. If mismatches occurred the likes of Stuart Pearce, Eddie Hapgood or Ramsey himself could be called to arms.

The final choice for Ramsey was who to play alongside Bobby Moore. Although Brian Clough left Moore out of his all-time England team, there was no chance that Ramsey would omit the man with whom his own managerial career is most closely associated. Composed and usually neat, Moore would battle with Beckenbauer, Baresi and Passarella for the title of the tournament's top defender. The battle to join Moore came to matter of taste. The (slightly over-inflated?) legend of Billy Wright; the extreme pace of Des Walker; the all-round ability of Roy McFarland; or the braveheart stopper Tony Adams? In the end, Ramsey bypassed them all and went for Moore's most famous partner, Jack Charlton. Not at the top of anyone's all-time great player list, but competent enough - at least until now.

Goalkeepers

Banks is generally regarded as one of the three best post-war goalkeepers (Yashin and Zoff being the others). His save from Pelé was a perfect encapsulation of a remarkable career. England had some fine players at the time but it's no coincidence that their finest hours (1966 and the semi-finals of the

17

European Championships in 1968) coincided with the presence of Banks in goal.

Shilton's international reputation isn't quite as strong, but more than 20 years at the top of the domestic game convinced many English observers that Shilts should be number one.

In the end Ramsey plumped for Banks, but no team would have a stronger goalkeeping representation than England's Banks, Shilton and Frank Swift (Czechoslovakia's Planicka, Viktor and Schroif might have come close had they made the finals).

Changes might be needed game by game, but most England fans were confident in the selection. Ramsey's confidence, of course, was never in doubt, though even he fell short of promising a World Cup win this time around.

Starting line-up (4-4-2)
Gordon Banks; Jimmy Armfield, Jack Charlton, Bobby Moore, Ray Wilson; Stanley Matthews, Duncan Edwards, Bobby Charlton, Tom Finney; Gary Lineker, Jimmy Greaves

ENGLAND WORLD CUP HISTORY

Year	Result	P	W	D	L
1930	Did not enter				
1934	Did not enter				
1938	Did not enter				
1950	Eliminated in round one	3	1	0	2
1954	Eliminated in quarter-finals	3	1	1	1
1958	Eliminated in round one	4	0	3	1
1962	Eliminated in quarter-finals	4	1	1	2
1966	Winners	6	5	1	0
1970	Eliminated in quarter-finals	4	2	0	2
1974	Did not qualify				
1978	Did not qualify				
1982	Eliminated in round two	5	3	2	0
1986	Eliminated in quarter-finals	5	2	1	2
1990	Eliminated in semi-finals (4th)	7	3	3*	1
1994	Did not qualify				
1998	Eliminated in round two	4	2	1*	1
Totals		**45**	**20**	**13**	**12**

*Lost one game on penalties

REPUBLIC OF IRELAND

When luck isn't enough

Before the late 1980s the Republic of Ireland somewhat under-achieved as an international team. Since 1988 the Irish have surpassed themselves, reaching three World Cups, including a quarter-final in 1990. The difference was Jack Charlton, the charismatic Englishman, who'd be the only man in tournament to represent one tournament as a player (England) and another as manager.

Forwards

Ireland's football in the last 15 years hasn't always been pretty. Charlton's direct approach made the most of the limited resources, and given the opposition in this tournament, Big Jack would once again need to turn water into wine. Essential to his plans would be a big target man. Niall Quinn and Tony Cascarino were Charlton's favourites, but their predecessor, Frank Stapleton, had a superior pedigree. A star for Arsenal and Manchester United, this would be his first World Cup experience despite 71 caps that yielded 20 goals.

Alongside Stapleton, Ireland would utilise John Aldridge, goal-poacher extraordinaire. Of course, like many of Charlton's recruits, Aldridge wasn't actually Irish, but he qualified through grandparents, and that was good enough for Jack. Young Robbie Keane, who looks set to surpass Quinn's national goal scoring record, would stand by as a replacement, but it was obvious that scoring goals would be Ireland's biggest headache.

Midfielders

The Republic's greatest-ever player would lead the team from midfield. Roy Keane's combination of power, aggression and football brain would be essential if the Irish were to tame more skilful sides. A Manchester United legend, Keane was slow to establish himself in the same way with Ireland, but once he did, he became his country's number one talisman. Keane would not lack for help in this team. Liam Brady, the sublimely skilled playmaker, made his name with Arsenal before seeking his fortune in Italy. He could paint a pretty picture with his left foot, and seemed an ideal counter-balance to the steely Keane. Johnny Giles was something of a Keane-Brady hybrid. Strong and feisty, but with great touch too, he'd be stationed out on the right in this side. He began his career on the wing for Manchester United before making his mark in the centre for Leeds, but the midfield threesome would be flexible enough not to limit Giles too

19

much. Steve Heighway only played 34 times for his national team and didn't get on the score sheet, but for his club side he was a revelation. The speedy winger represented a major weapon in Liverpool's attacking arsenal in the 1970s, and surrounded by similarly talented team mates, Charlton hoped to translate his club form onto the big stage.

Ronnie Whelan, another Liverpool stalwart, and Scottish-born winger Ray Houghton would act as cover, but Charlton was aware that if his front line failed to deliver the reserve troops were unlikely to do any better.

Defenders

Ireland's success in the 90s was built on the determined obstinacy of their defence. Paul McGrath - the focal point of the 1990 and 1994 sides - and one of the great central-defenders of his age, played most of his international football in midfield. Charlton perceived him too important to use in defence in the 1990s, but given the increased options of the All-Time side, McGrath reverted to his more familiar position. Alongside him would be Mark Lawrenson. Liverpool's smooth defender played just 38 times for Ireland and never in the World Cup. He'd relish the opportunity to show his mettle against the very best. The full-back positions were filled by Denis Irwin and John Carey. Irwin was a dependable part of Manchester United's dominant team in the 1990s and featured for his national team in 1994. He was challenged for a place by Steve Staunton, but his extensive European experience gave Irwin the edge. Carey was unchallenged at right-back after an impressive career in which he led the famous post-war Manchester United side. Arguably the greatest full-back produced in the British Isles, he'd enjoy a reunion with wingers such as Finney and Matthews.

Goalkeepers

There were one or two positions where the Republic might have wanted to borrow from their Irish neighbours to the north. George Best stands out, but an even greater need was in goal. Pat Jennings or Elisha Scott would have helped enormously, as the choice of custodians was rather thin. Charlton would rely on Pat Bonner once again, but no one was really convinced.

That Ireland made it this far was something of an achievement, but to go any further would take a rather large dose of Irish luck. Jack would motivate and organise, but it was unlikely to be enough.

Roy Keane

Manchester United have boasted some fine defensive midfielders over the years. From Duncan Edwards and Nobby Stiles, to Bryan Robson and Paul Ince, it seems there's always been a powerful presence in the Red Devils' engine room. Despite such illustrious predecessors, however, there are now many United experts who claim that Roy Keane has surpassed them all.

Having started his career in Ireland with Cobb Ramblers, Keane was snapped up by Brian Clough's Nottingham Forrest in 1990. Some dynamic displays led to rave reviews and in 1993, United, the newly crowned English champions, signed him for £3.75m.

With Keane on board United went on to dominate the decade. In his first year, United claimed the double. A fallow year in 1995 was followed by another double in 1996 and a third title the following year. By now, United had embraced a new generation of exciting youngsters and Keane matured into the team's forceful leader. His style changed slightly too. Having been a regular goal scorer in his early days, he began to sit back more and dictate the game from midfield. With his combination of powerful tackling, forceful leadership and clever distribution he became his team's focal point.

In 1999, United finally regained the European Cup as they won an unprecedented treble. Unfortunately for Keane he missed the European Final through suspension having made a colossal contribution as captain en route. Two more league titles followed for United as Keane came to be recognised as the best player of his type anywhere in the world.

Although Keane's name has been made as the driving force of United, he's had his moments for Ireland too. Some critics felt he failed to assert himself fully early in his international career, but by the end of the 90s, it was clear that Ireland's fortunes depended to a large extent on the gigantic influence of their captain. Having played in all four games in the 1994 World Cup, in which his team shocked Italy on its way to the second round, Keane was instrumental as Ireland overcame a tough group to qualify for its third finals tournament in 2002.

Starting-line-up (4-4-2)
Pat Bonner; John Carey, Paul McGrath, Mark Lawrenson, Denis Irwin; Johnny Giles, Roy Keane, Liam Brady, Steve Heighway; John Aldridge, Frank Stapleton

REPUBLIC OF IRELAND WORLD CUP HISTORY

Year	Result	P	W	D	L
1930	Did not enter				
1934	Did not enter				
1938	Did not enter				
1950	Did not qualify				
1954	Did not qualify				
1958	Did not qualify				
1962	Did not qualify				
1966	Did not qualify				
1970	Did not qualify				
1974	Did not qualify				
1978	Did not qualify				
1982	Did not qualify				
1986	Did not qualify				
1990	Eliminated in Quarter Finals	5	0	4*	1
1994	Eliminated in round two	4	1	1	2
1998	Did not qualify				
Totals		9	1	5	3

*Won one game on penalties

SWEDEN

Organised over-achievers

George Raynor was the undisputed choice as Swedish coach. Arguably the most successful of all English-born coaches, Raynor led Sweden to a World Cup semi-final in 1950 and a Final in 1958. Had the Swedes allowed overseas-based players to participate earlier, Raynor might have found a way to challenge in 1954 too. Most of his side would be drawn from the golden 1950s era (actually it started in 1948 with the Olympic gold medal). The great Gren-Nordahl-Liedholm (Grenoli) trinity of AC Milan fame would all challenge for places, as would several other Italian exports.

Forwards

The options were plentiful up front, with some of the most prolific marksmen of all-time looking for a spot. Gunnar Nordahl scored 43 goals in 33 internationals during the 1940s and later for Milan netted 225 times in 257 Italian games, a phenomenal rate even for the 1950s. Sven Rydell's rate was hardly less impressive, 49 goals in 43 internationals during the 1920s and 1930s. Not to be sneered at, even if many were plundered against emerging nations like Finland and Norway. Agne Simonson had been the main striker in the 1958 side and was worthy of consideration, while the likes of Ove Kindvall, Kennet Andersson and Ralf Edström had also served their country well. In the end, Raynor chose to add a dash of flair to the power of Nordahl and plumped for little Tomas Brolin, who always seemed to be either over or under-rated, but produced some fine performances when it mattered most.

Midfielders

Kurt Hamrin starred in Italy and was a devastating right-winger. Small, but quick and elusive, he was one of the key factors in Sweden's run to the final in the World Cup of 1958, scoring a fine goal in the semi-final victory over the West Germans. Latter day hero Anders Limpar was available too, but he was never in the same class. Lennart Skoglund started as an inside forward and was one of the key forces in the 1950 side. He really blossomed, however, once he moved to the left wing and was the only outfield player to play in both the 1950 and 1958 teams.

Between the wings, Sweden had some difficult choices to make. Gunnar Gren and Nils Liedholm were great inside forwards and were chosen to start, but as a pair seemed to lack bite. Other options included Jonas Thern and Stefan Schwarz, who'd combined so effectively in the 1994 semi-final team, and Karl-Erik Palmér who did well in 1950. Neither Thern or Palmér added much in the way of power, and the idea of Schwarz at this level didn't sit quite right. Raynor could also turn to Bo Larsson, a fine playmaker in the 1970s who had a 15-year career with the national team.

Defenders

At the back, a pair of Nilssons challenged at full-back. Erik, the captain in 1950, got the start on the left but Roland, who played for many years in England, lost out to Orvar Bergmark, one of the best right-backs in the world in 1950s.

Between them, the man Welsh legend John Charles rated as the best he'd

Gunnar Nordahl

For Degerfors and Norrkoping in Sweden, for AC Milan and Roma in Italy, and even for Sweden at international level, Gunnar Nordahl simply couldn't stop scoring goals.

An immensely strong centre-forward, he scored 43 goals in internationals between 1942 and 1948, culminating in Olympic gold in London. Nordahl scored seven times in four Olympic fixtures, including one in the Final against Yugoslavia.

His goal-scoring feats, which included 77 goals in 58 games for Degerfors and 93 in 92 for Norrkoping, attracted the attention of Milan, who would not be disappointed.

Nordahl became easily the most successful foreign player in Italian football to that time, and ranks among the greatest of all Italian imports. Forming a deadly front-line with fellow Swedes Gunnar Gren and Nils Liedholm, Nordahl soon went to work on Italy's finest defences.

In eight seasons with Milan, he was five times the league's top scorer - including 35 in 1949-50 - which remains a record for a 38-game season. He notched up 34 in 37 matches the following season. In total there were 210 goals for Milan and two Scudettos (championships).

Incredibly, Nordahl's 15 goals in 34 games for Roma marked the least fertile scoring spell of his career. In all, the former fireman (he was nicknamed "Pompiere") scored 225 times in 257 Italian league matches, easily the best strike rate of all-time.

It seemed that Nordahl was simply too strong for his opponents, but there was one who prevented him scoring goals - the Swedish FA. Due to Sweden's policy of not picking professionals for the national team, Nordahl didn't play international football after 1948. Given his strike rate it seems reasonable to assume that he would have challenged Puskas's record of 83 international goals had he continued to play for the national team. Indeed, it's possible that with Nordahl, Gren and the others, Sweden might have mounted a real challenge to Hungary (and West Germany) in the 1954 World Cup.

Sadly, Nordahl retired in 1957, which meant he was unable to join the other exiles for Sweden's run to the World Cup Final in 1958. It was the world's loss that it never got to see one the greatest marksmen of all do his thing at the highest level.

faced, Bengt Gustavsson was paired with Bjorn Nordquist, who was capped 115 times without scoring a single goal.

Goalkeepers
Sweden were another team with a good choice of custodians. The flamboyant Thomas Ravelli or Karl Svensson could have done the job, but Ronnie Hellström had the edge.

The Swedish side would lack some of the superstars boasted by other teams, but there would be no real weak links, and as with all Raynor sides, they'd be organised and motivated.

Starting line-up (4-4-2)
Ronnie Hellström; Orvar Bergmark, Bjorn Nordquist, Bengt Gustavsson, Erik Nilsson; Kurt Hamrin, Nils Liedholm, Gunnar Gren, Lennart Skoglund; Gunnar Nordahl, Tomas Brolin

SWEDEN WORLD CUP HISTORY

Year	Result	P	W	D	L
1930	Did not enter				
1934	Eliminated in quarter-finals	2	1	0	1
1938	Eliminated in semi-finals (4th)	3	1	0	2
1950	Eliminated in Final Phase (3rd)	5	2	1	2
1954	Did not qualify				
1958	Lost in Final	6	4	1	1
1962	Did not qualify				
1966	Did not qualify				
1970	Eliminated in round one	3	1	1	1
1974	Eliminated in round two	6	2	2	2

1978	Eliminated in round one	3	0	1	2
1982	Did not qualify				
1986	Did not qualify				
1990	Eliminated in round one	3	0	0	3
1994	Eliminated in semi-finals	7	3	3*	1
1998	Did not qualify				
Total		**38**	**14**	**9**	**15**

*Won one game on penalties

AUSTRIA

Wunderfull, then woeful

Hugo Meisl, coach of the "Wunderteam" of the 1930s, would lead the All-Time side. Widely considered one of football's great pioneers, Meisl brought a wise head to an Austrian side that would need all the help it could get.

Austria's qualification was a surprise to many, but they twice made the World Cup semi-finals and might have done even better had they competed in either 1930 or 1950.

Forwards

Austria had several worthy choices up front. Josef Bican, born in Vienna, and raised by Czech parents, played first for Austria and then for Czechoslovakia. For Austria he formed a great partnership with Matthias Sindelar in the 1934 World Cup and scored 14 international goals. He scored a further 12 for Czechoslovakia between 1938 and 1949. Bican's peak years came during World War II when he scored 229 goals in the Czech league.

Franz Binder, another 1930s legend, was one of the most prolific marksmen of all-time. Like Bican he peaked during the war and won only 19 Austrian caps between 1934 and 1947, knocking in 16 goals. He also scored 10 in nine appearances for Germany.

Challenging Binder and Bican were two modern goal machines. Hans Krankl scored a cool 34 in 69 internationals during the 1970s and 1980s, and scored at World Cup level too. Toni Polster scored 44 goals in 95 caps over a 19-year period, but his record of one goal in six World Cup matches counted against him. Another "Wunderteam" member, Anton Schall, only added to Austria's strength in depth.

Meisl opted for something old and something new in Binder and Krankl but it seemed unthinkable that Bican wouldn't force his way in at some point.

26

Ernst Ocwirk

Together with Obdulio Varela, Ernst "Clockwork" Ocwirk was the last of the great attacking centre-halves. Austria didn't adapt to the stopper centre-back system until long after most of their European rivals, which meant that during the 1950s they were both uniquely attack-minded and extremely vulnerable.

Ocwirk was first capped in 1947 and went on to win 62 caps spread out over 15 years. Following a poor showing in the 1948 Olympics, Austria quickly improved and were soon one of the best teams in Europe; at least until Hungary emerged as the dominant force. Even then, Austria were competitive and had arguably the best record against the Magic Magyars. Between 1950 and 1953 Austria played their neighbours four times, winning one, drawing one and losing two, but never by more than a single goal. Consequently, when the draw for the 1954 World Cup kept Hungary and Austria apart, many expected a showdown in the Final.

It never happened as Ocwirk's team were hammered 6-1 by a physical

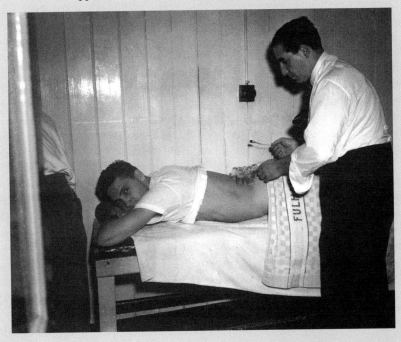

West Germany, the eventual champions, in the semis. This was a surprise, but spoke to the antiquated system that Austria employed. With Ocwirk and his fellow half-backs - which at various times included Gerhard Hanappi and Karl Koller - as concerned with attack as they were with defence, Austria would always be a threat going forward, but leaked goals as well. In five matches in Switzerland they scored 17 goals but conceded 12. The 7-5 quarter-final victory over Switzerland said it all.

Even in defeat Ocwirk stood out and he signed off from the World Cup with a goal in the third-place play-off, a 3-1 win over the fancied Uruguayans.

Ocwirk was selected as a wing-half for the Rest of the World Team that played England in 1953 and, three years later, moved to Italy where he played five seasons for Sampdoria.

Midfielders

The team's focal point would be Ernst Ocwirk, one of the great attacking centre-halves. Ocwirk's case is a good illustration of the problems faced in selecting players from half a century ago. The tactics of today's game bear little resemblance to those of pre-1960 or so. That Ocwirk's position is given the same name as that played by Tony Adams, for instance, is little more than coincidence. Ocwirk operated much as a modern midfielder would. A strong presence in defence, but also a creative force in attack and the hub around which his team was built.

Meisl would therefore set Ocwirk to work in central midfield. Matthias Sindelar, another Austrian icon would keep him company. A centre-forward in the 1930s side, Sindelar is another who defies the current interpretation of his position. Meisl's favourite son was a deep lying playmaker, but with bite as well.

If Austria required reinforcement they could call on Herbert Prohaska, a talented ball player in the 1970s, or Karl Koller, a fine left-half who won 86 caps from 1952 to 1965. Josef Smistik, centre-half in 1934, was another who'd be best employed in midfield. Andreas Herzog has been one of the few bright sparks for Austria over the last decade but was unlikely to unseat his illustrious predecessors.

Out wide on the right, Meisl called on Franz Hasil. An important contributor to the fine Feyenoord side of the early 1970s, Hasil represented Austria just 21 times over an 11-year period, mainly because the Austrian selectors shied away from picking players with foreign clubs.

Complementing Hasil on the left wing would be Alfred Körner. A World

Cup semi-finalist in 1954, Körner was a dangerous winger in the national side for over a decade and a vital force behind Austria's 7-5 win over Switzerland in the quarter-finals. Körner's brother Robert was also important and the right-winger would act as a reserve for Hasil.

Defenders

The Austrian defence wasn't any easier for Meisl to fathom. Great half-back Ernst Happel would play centre-back and be joined by national team stalwart Bruno Pezzey. Sweeper Erich Obermayer would stand by.

Robert Sara, a contemporary of both Pezzey and Obermayer in the 1970s, would start at right-back where the options seemed more limited.

The left-back position was a particular problem but luckily Meisl could call upon perhaps the most versatile international player ever. Gerhard Hanappi won 93 caps in nine different positions for Austria and would slot in where needed. Karl Koller could probably fill in if necessary.

Goalkeepers

Fritz Koncilia, a national fixture in goal for 16 years would start between the posts, though many expected Meisl to turn to the familiar Rudi Hiden at the first hint of trouble.

For a country that once went 20 years between World Cup finals appearances, Meisl's squad looked pretty strong. Not tournament winners, but certainly no pushovers either. Their opening match with Germany would spark a few emotions.

Starting line-up (4-4-2)
Fritz Koncilla; Robert Sara, Bruno Pezzey, Ernst Happel, Gerhard Hanappi; Franz Hasil, Ernst Ocwirk, Matthias Sindelar, Albert Korner; Franz Binder, Hans Krankl

AUSTRIA WORLD CUP HISTORY

Year	Resul	P	W	D	L
1930	Did not enter				
1934	Eliminated in semi-finals	4	2	0	2
1938	Did not enter				
1950	Did not enter				
1954	Eliminated in semi-finals	5	4	0	1

1958	Eliminated in round one	3	0	1	2
1962	Did not qualify				
1966	Did not qualify				
1970	Did not qualify				
1974	Did not qualify				
1978	Eliminated in round two	6	3	0	3
1982	Eliminated in round two	5	2	1	2
1986	Did not qualify				
1990	Eliminated in round one	3	1	0	2
1994	Did not qualify				
1998	Eliminated in round one	3	0	2	1
Total		**29**	**12**	**4**	**13**

FRANCE

Matching style with substance

Aime Jacquet led France to their first World Cup triumph in 1998, and would be charged with producing similar results this time.

Forwards

Just Fontaine scored 13 goals in the 1958 World Cup. Playing as a lone striker in front of some fine French midfielders, he looked set to bag a few more. The five-man midfield employed by Jacquet left no room for two or three other fine strikers. Jean-Pierre Papin and Eric Cantona were of the highest class, although critics argued they'd failed to even qualify for the World Cup finals in 1994. Roger Piantoni played alongside Kopa, Fontaine and Jean Vincent in 1958, but wasn't so lucky this time.

Midfielders

The resources seemed especially plentiful in midfield. Jacquet's main task was to integrate three great playmakers into one fearsome side. Raymond Kopa was the key figure in France's first World Cup run. Kopa's promptings in 1958 led France to the semi-finals and earned him the title of European Footballer of the Year. Kopa won three European Cups with Real Madrid and was commonly regarded the greatest French player until the arrival of Michel Platini. Between the demise of Cruyff and the rise of Maradona, Platini was the world's best player and three-times European Footballer of the Year. He was captain of the

30

great French side of the 1980s that reached the World Cup semi-finals twice and won the 1984 European title in some style.

Zinedine Zidane has mounted a serious challenge to Platini's throne, providing the major creative force in the side that followed its World Cup triumph with a European Championship.

Although some questioned whether all three could co-exist, Jacquet insisted that he'd try to make them gel. Kopa was pushed slightly to the right (where he started his career), Zidane moved left, leaving Platini in the middle. There'd certainly be no shortage of creativity.

Didier Deschamps was chosen to anchor the midfield and attempt to win the ball for his three maestros. Luis Fernandez and Emmanuel Petit were also considered, but Jacquet stuck with Deschamps' leadership skills. Jean Tigana completed the midfield. A smooth operator and not a traditional ball-winner, he'd be cast in a supporting role here.

At least he made the side. Alan Giresse, Youri Djorkaeff, and wingers Didier Six and Jean Vincent, weren't so lucky.

Defenders

There was depth of choice in defence too, and Jacquet could call upon one the greatest defensive units ever assembled (by Jacquet himself in 1998 as it happens). Lilian Thuram on the right, Bixente Lizarazu on the left, with Laurent Blanc and Marcel Desailly in the middle had looked practically impregnable in helping France lift the World Cup. All but the amazing Desailly faced serious competition for their places however. Jocelyn Angloma, Patrick Battiston and particularly Manuel Amoros would challenge Thuram. Maxime Bossis would threaten Lizarazu's place as would Roger Marche, another veteran of 1958. Blanc, who missed out on the World Cup Final due to suspension, lost out to 1958 star Robert Jonquet for the sweeper role.

Goalkeepers

Joel Bats, the keeper in the 1980s, and World Cup winner Fabian Barthez would face off for the keeper's jersey. Barthez, as skillful with the ball at his feet as many outfield players, was more flamboyant, but Jacquet would try Bats first. Bernard Lama, Barthez's long-time rival would complete the goalkeeping compliment, which looked a little light-weight by the standards of this tournament.

All in all, it was an exciting side. Skill and power in equal measure and a prolific marksman to put the icing on the cake. Assuming Jacquet could keep every one pulling in the same direction, a serious challenge looked likely.

Starting line-up (4-2-3-1)
Joel Bats; Lilian Thuram, Marcel Desailly, Robert Jonquet, Maxime Bossis; Jean Tigana, Didier Deschamps; Raymond Kopa, Michel Platini, Zinedine Zidane; Just Fontaine

FRANCE WORLD CUP HISTORY

Year	Result	P	W	D	L
1930	Eliminated in round one	3	1	0	2
1934	Eliminated in round one	1	0	0	1
1938	Eliminated in quarter-finals	2	1	0	1
1950	Did not qualify				
1954	Eliminated in round one	2	1	0	1
1958	Eliminated in semi-finals (3rd)	6	4	0	2
1962	Did not qualify				
1966	Eliminated in round one	3	0	1	2
1970	Did not qualify				
1974	Did not qualify				
1978	Eliminated in round one	3	1	0	2
1982	Eliminated in semi-finals (4th)	7	3	2*	2
1986	Eliminated in semi-finals (3rd)	7	4	2**	1
1990	Did not qualify				
1994	Did not qualify				
1998	Champions	7	6	1**	0
Total		**41**	**21**	**6**	**14**

*Lost one game on penalties
**Won one game on penalties

GERMANY

Consistent quality and performance

Franz Beckenbauer, the only man to both captain and coach a World Cup winner, was a strong candidate to coach the All-Time team, but gave way to Helmut Schön, who led West Germany in four World Cups, guiding them to the trophy in 1974, second place in 1966 and third spot in 1970. Beckenbauer was a key player on each occasion, and would again be the team's focal point.

Germany had one of the strongest pools of players to choose from, drawing on stars from the dominant West German teams as well as the less successful East German and unified German sides.

Forwards

Up front, Schön decided on a three-man unit - a central striker surrounded by two wingers. This classic German formation made things extremely competitive in the middle, although challengers for the left-hand spot seemed rather scarce. Jürgen Klinsmann and Uwe Seeler were two of the finest strikers ever and scorers of 20 World Cup goals between them but were merely reserves. East Germany's greatest player, Joachim Streich, would keep them company. Gerd Müller, commonly regarded as the finest goal scorer of them all, would be Schön's first choice, and it was hard to disagree.

Whether Klinsmann, Streich or Seeler could have played alongside Der Bomber in place of the left-winger was open to debate. Pierre Littbarski, fine player that he was, looked a little out of place in this side, so Schön moved Helmut Rahn over from the right. Big and powerful but highly skilled, Rahn had been one of the most memorable players in both 1954 and 1958, scoring several miraculous goals. He'd roam across the front line and Schön might not always know what to expect - but neither would the opposition.

Karl-Heinz Rummenigge would play on the right wing as he did early in his career. He later became one of Europe's finest strikers so Schön wouldn't expect his man to hug the touchline. Jürgen Grabowski, torturer of Terry Cooper in 1970, would act as back-up, assuming he held off Thomas Hassler and Siggi Held.

Midfielders

Lothar Matthäus was the only sure thing in midfield. One hundred and fifty caps and five World Cups saw to that. An all-rounder who also later played sweeper, he'd form a fearsome partnership with Beckenbauer, or just about anyone else.

33

The leading candidates to join him were Fritz Walter, who's 18-year career as a composed playmaker encompassed lifting the World Cup in 1954, Wolfgang Overath, and two maverick geniuses. Günter Netzer had forced his way past Overath to star in arguably West Germany's greatest team - the one that lifted the 1972 European Championship. His star fell as quickly as it rose, injury not helping his cause, but he'd certainly add a dash of the unpredictable to Schön's line-up. Bernd Schuster was cast in a similar mould. Star of the 1980 European Champions, Schuster never participated in a World Cup after falling out with team management, but lit up the Spanish league for many years. East German Gerd Weber, who attempted to flee to the West, and Helmut Haller, would warm the bench.

Defenders

Schön's choice in defence was formidable. Berti Vogts, Cruyff's nemesis in 1974, was the obvious choice at right-back, even if Manfred Katz, and 1930s legend Paul Janes, were also strong candidates. The left-back spot was even more crowded. Andreas Brehme of stunning free kick fame was favourite, but what about Karl-Heinz Schnellinger, a powerful presence in four World Cups? Paul Breitner was also considered here and challenged in midfield too.

In the centre of defence, much depended on Beckenbauer, the greatest sweeper of all-time. If Schön elected to play him in his most famous role, then the battle for the remaining spot in defence would be fierce. Karl-Heinz Förster, Jürgen Kohler and Willy Schulz all had their champions. Schulz was a favourite of Kenneth Wolstenholme in 1966, but Förster got Schön's initial vote. Of course, if Beckenbauer returned to midfield, former East German Matthias Sammer, who stood out in Euro 96, would be a strong favourite to slot in as sweeper, although Schulz would be comfortable there too.

Goalkeepers

The arguments were perhaps fiercest in goal. Sepp Maier was one of the great World Cup keepers, a key figure in 1974, but there were those who questioned his consistency on the lesser stage. Schön reasoned that there would be no bigger arena than this so he took his chances, which made sense but was hard on a couple of others. Jürgen Croy kept a clean sheet for East Germany on the only occasion the two Germanys met (East Germany won 1-0). In all, he won 94 caps and was one of the best in the world for much of the 1970s. The same can be said about West Germany's Harald Schumacher in the 1980s, although many remember him best for his horrific challenge on Patrick Battiston in the 1982 World Cup.

THE CONTENDERS

The German team (all West German as it happens) looked formidable. Plenty of goal-scorers and goal-stoppers, several playmakers, and more than anything - a whole host of winners. The starting line-up had all won either a World Cup or European Championship. They'd be serious contenders to add to those honours here.

Starting line-up (4-3-3)
Sepp Maier; Berti Vogts, Karlheinz Förster, Franz Beckenbauer, Andreas Brehme; Lothar Matthäus, Fritz Walter, Wolfgang Overath; Karl-Heinz Rummenigge, Gerd Müller, Helmut Rahn

GERMANY WORLD CUP HISTORY

Year	Result	P	W	D	L
1930	Did not enter				
1934	Eliminated in semi-finals (3rd)	4	3	0	1
1938	Eliminated in round one	2	0	1	1
1950	Did not enter				
1954	Champions	6	5	0	1
1958	Eliminated in semi-finals (4th)	6	2	2	2
1962	Eliminated in quarter-finals	4	2	1	1
1966	Lost in Final	6	4	1	1
1970	Eliminated in semi-finals (3rd)	6	5	0	1
1974	(West) Champions	7	6	0	1
1974	(East) Eliminated in round two	6	2	2	2
1978	Eliminated in round two	6	1	4	1
1982	Lost in Final	7	3	2*	2
1986	Lost in Final	7	3	2*	2
1990	Champions	7	5	2*	0
1994	Eliminated in quarter-finals	5	3	1	1
1998	Eliminated in quarter-finals	5	3	1	1
Total		**84**	**47**	**19**	**18**

* Won one game on penalties
# Germany 1934-1938, 1994-1998; West Germany 1950-1990, East Germany reached finals only in 1974

SPAIN

Under-achievers or over-rated?

In the absence of any distinguished World Cup coach, Spain chose José Villalonga, who led Spain to their only major trophy - the 1964 European Championship. Javier Clemente, who had some success in the 1990s, was also considered, but the candidates weren't exactly clamouring for this poisoned chalice.

While Spanish clubs have consistently prospered in European competition, the national team has disappointed time and again. Just one World Cup semi-final appearance (in 1950) for a country with one of the strongest leagues in the world. Still, despite the let-downs, Spain could still call on some fine players.

A number of stars of the Spanish team would not be available, however. Under the rules of this competition, Alfredo Di Stefano, Ladislav Kubala and José Santamaria were all ruled out. Each would have been valuable, especially the goal scoring talents of Di Stefano and Kubala. Spain's all-time top scorer is defender Fernando Hierro.

Forwards

Emilio Butragueno and Zarra were charged with scoring the goals for Spain. "The Vulture" scored five in the 1986 World Cup and many more for Real Madrid, but 26 in 69 caps didn't stand comparison with Müller or Fontaine. Zarra's 20 in 20 certainly did, and the main force in 1950 would have to be on form again to give Spain a chance.

One day the exciting Raul might assume the mantle of Spain's greatest goal scorer, and the skilled forward would be a leading candidate to step into the breach should Zarra and Butragueno struggle.

Midfielders

On the right wing would be Michel, Real Madrid starlet and one of Spain's best players during the late 1980s. Estanislao Basora had been one of the best outside rights during the 1950 World Cup, and his 13 goals in 22 internationals spoke of a much-needed scoring touch. Selection was tight, but Michel's famous name would give opponents more to worry over. The famous Amancio Amorro was often exiled on the right wing but would also act as cover for the attacking midfield role.

First choice playmaker was Luis Suárez. An Inter Milan legend, Suárez was never the same force in internationals (which Spaniard was?) but is widely considered one of his country's finest products. Another 1990s golden boy, Josep Guardiola, would be the first choice holding player, although Victor Munoz was also considered. Real Madrid stalwart Pirri could cover several positions including centre-back and centre-midfield.

Fellow Real Madrid legend Francisco Gento strode into the side on the left wing, despite competition from the gifted Rafael Gordillo and Agustin Gainza - one of the 1950s greats.

Gento was electrifying in his heyday, and would severely test two of the great right-backs (Vogts and Thuram) in the group matches.

Francisco Gento

Real Madrid teammate Ferenc Puskas said that Gento was a more consistently dangerous attacker on the left wing than even the great Hungarian Zoltan Czibor, which was quite a compliment, but well deserved.

Gento signed for Real in 1953 and finally retired in 1971 having played 761 matches and scored over 250 goals. In many ways, Gento, and not his famous team mate Alfredo Di Stefano, was the quintessential Real player.

The team won 12 Spanish Championships during Gento's stay and only he has won six European Cups, the first five with Di Stefano and then again in 1966.

Armed with exceptional pace, ball skills and a marvellous footballing brain, Gento was probably the finest left-winger of his day. Only Mário Zagallo and Czibor come close. Unlike Di Stefano, Gento did have the opportunity to display his talents in the World Cup, but found little joy.

Although he won 43 caps and scored five goals over a 14-year period and played in two World Cups, Spain never lifted any trophies with Gento in the side. The winger was strangely omitted when Spain won the European Championship in 1964.

Although questions are asked about Spain's under-achieving after every major competition, never were the questions more apt than during Gento's time. Surely a team that at various times could draw upon imports like Puskas, Kubala, Santamaria and Di Stefano, as well as the talents of Luis Suárez and Gento, should have been able to get past Scotland to qualify for the 1958 World Cup, or progress beyond the first round in 1962. Even as reigning European Champions in 1966 they failed to make an impact. A front line including Luis Del Sol, Suárez, Amancio Amaro, Joaquim Peiró and Gento could muster only four goals in one win and two defeats.

It was hard on Gento, who vies with Suárez as the greatest Spanish-born outfield player, but at least he has all those European Cups as consolation.

Defenders

Hierro would form part of the team's core and would be joined in defence by Antonio Maceda, a big blonde sweeper who had looked good in the European Championships of 1984 before being cut down by injury. There were other contenders; Manuel Sanchis and Nadal among them, but Villalonga seemed happy enough with his pairing which was both skilled and strong.

The battle for the left-back spot came down to Sergi and José Camacho. Sergi, a star of Barcelona, was brilliant going forward, while Camacho was sounder in defence. Villalonga looked at the left flank and decided defence was the greater need. Juan Segarra would provide extra insurance even though he only won 25 caps over an 11-year period.

The choice on the right was less formidable. Feliciano Rivilla held the spot for Spain during the relatively successful early 1960s, but was no great. Chendo was Spain's choice in the late 1980s and Chelsea's Albert Ferrer was the man of the 1990s. None of them looked like striking fear into the slew of quality left-

THE CONTENDERS

wingers that awaited in the tournament but Villalonga plumped for Ferrer and crossed his fingers.

Goalkeepers

One area of strength for Spain was in goal. Ricardo Zamora, the greatest keeper of the pre-war years, got the start - there was no question about that - but Villalonga had a number of worthy back-ups. Andoni Zubizarreta won 126 caps in the 1980s and 1990s and Antonio Ramallets wore Spain's number one jersey from 1950 to 1961.

The Spanish side looked competitive, if not exactly overwhelming. Many expected the usual World Cup implosion. Villalonga hoped otherwise.

Starting line-up (4-4-2)
Ricardo Zamora; Albert Ferrer, Fernando Hierro, Antonio Maceda, José Camacho; Michel, Josep Guardiola, Luis Suárez, Francisco Gento; Emilio Butragueno, Zarra

SPAIN WORLD CUP HISTORY

Year	Result	P	W	D	L
1930	Did not enter				
1934	Eliminated in round two	3	1	1	1
1938	Did not enter				
1950	Eliminated in semi-finals	6	3	1	2
1954	Did not qualify				
1958	Did not qualify				
1962	Eliminated in round one	3	1	0	2
1966	Eliminated in round one	3	1	0	2
1970	Did not qualify				
1974	Did not qualify				
1978	Eliminated in round one	3	1	1	1
1982	Eliminated in round two	5	1	2	2
1986	Eliminated in quarter-finals	5	3	1*	1
1990	Eliminated in round two	4	2	1	1
1994	Eliminated in quarter-finals	5	2	2	1
1998	Eliminated in round one	3	1	1	1
Total		**40**	**16**	**10**	**14**

* Lost one game on penalties

HUNGARY

Magic and decline

Hungarian football is synonymous with the great team of the early 1950s. Gusztáv Sebes was in charge of that side, and was the only candidate as boss of the All-Time team. The "Magic Magyars", as Sebes' team was called, would contribute the nucleus of the select side, but there were several other greats to be considered too.

Forwards

Sebes started with Ferenc Puskas - with the exception of Diego Maradona - the greatest of all left-footed players. Puskas dominated European football for over a decade, first with Hungary and then with Real Madrid. Any team hoping to stop Hungary would first have to put a hold on the "Galloping Major".

Puskas' striking partner in the team that won the Olympic Gold in 1952 and lost in the 1954 World Cup Final, was Sándor Kocsis, who scored an astounding 75 goals in 68 internationals.

Kocsis was not without rivals for a place in this team, however. Hungary has produced an incredible array of goal scorers. In 1938, when they reached the World Cup Final, the team's top man was Györgi Sárosi, an old fashioned centre-forward who also played centre-half. He scored 42 goals in 61 internationals, so obviously fitted the striker's bill, but Sebes could also use him in midfield. Sárosi's partner at inside-left was Gyula Zsengellér, who once scored five goals in a World Cup qualifier. Sárosi and Zsengellér followed several early superstars of European football such as Imre Schlosser-Lakatos, Kalman Konrad, Alfred Schaffer and Gyorgy Orth.

In the 1940s, a new inside-forward superstar emerged. Ladislav Kubala might have been a key player in the 1950s team had he not fled west. He eventually joined Barcelona, where he flourished into one of Europe's finest, and played 19 times for Spain (he also won caps for Czechoslovakia). In the 1960s, Lajos Tichy developed as a top class goal scorer. Big and strong, he piled in 49 goals in 71 games.

Sebes decided to start with Puskas and Kocsis, but he wasn't exactly short of cover.

Ferenc Puskas

Puskas was the greatest player of his day, and up to that point, the greatest player of any day.

Puskas joined his local club, Kispest, at the age of 16 and two years later he'd found his way into the national side. Hungary were one of the better teams in Europe before World War II, but Puskas helped turn them into the most dominant team of all-time. Hungary went unbeaten in 32 consecutive matches from 1950 and were Olympic Champions in 1952. The run came to an end in the 1954 World Cup Final. Hungary were heavy favourites, especially having beaten rivals West Germany 8-3 in the group stage, including a marvellous solo effort from Puskas. But more important than the win was the injury sustained to Puskas. The great man sat out the next two matches - the infamous Battle of Berne and the great encounter with Uruguay - but he was back for the Final. He made an immediate impact, scoring the opening goal after just six minutes, but West Germany weren't intimidated like many other teams and finally clawed their way back. The loss remains the greatest upset in World Cup Final history.

Hungary remained a dominant side until 1956 and in all Puskas scored 83 goals in 84 matches for the Magic Magyars.

The Hungarian Revolution brought an end to the era, as many key players defected to the west. Honved, the army club side for which Puskas now played, went on a European tour during the first phase of the October Uprising, and later travelled to South America as Russian tanks crushed the rebellion. Although some players returned to Hungary, Puskas decided against returning home. Instead he made his way to Italy where he waited out an 18-month ban imposed by FIFA at the request of the Hungarian FA.

Many clubs weren't interested in signing a 31-year old, but Real Madrid, already European Champions, decided to take a chance. In Madrid, Puskas teamed up with Alfredo Di Stefano and an exceptional side became all but unbeatable. In 1960, Madrid won their fifth European Cup with a 7-3 thrashing of Eintracht Frankfurt in the Final. Puskas scored four and Di Stefano three as Madrid put on possibly the finest ever display of attacking football.

In 1962, Puskas returned to the World Cup Finals where he represented Spain, but an unsettled side were eliminated in round one.

Heavy around the middle, no right foot - they don't sound like the credentials for an all-time great. But a fine footballing brain and his left foot - the single greatest weapon in football history - helped Puskas thrive in two great sides, and cement his place as one of the true icons of the game.

Midfielders

By comparison, Sebe's other decisions were simple, but they evoked some intriguing discussions.

The "Magic Magyars" not only had immense talent, they also unveiled a new tactic. Sebes played Nándor Hidegkuti, an inside forward by trade, as a deep-lying centre-forward. The move caused havoc against England in 1953, when the English centre-half Harry Johnston didn't know who to mark. Sebes is sometimes given credit for inventing this tactic, but in fact he simply perfected it for the national team. It was Marton Bukovi, Hidegkuti's trainer at club side MTK, who first developed the strategy of using the number nine as a creative midfielder.

Hidegkuti was an obvious candidate to fill the playmaker's role in the All-Time side, but he had a formidable rival. Florian Albert was the key member of the 1960s team that twice made the World Cup quarter-finals. Another deep-lying centre-forward, Albert regularly took over games, and Sebes hoped he could do so again. Lajos Detari, a playmaker in the 1980s and the last world class Hungarian player, would act as second reserve.

On the wings, Sebes chose 1950s star Zoltán Czibor, and Albert's cohort Ferenc Bene. Both were quick and skilled, both were world-beaters. Sándor Zambo, who looked good in the 1972 European Championships, covered on the left. Tibor Nyilasi, a great, but often disappointing, talent in the late 1970s, backed up Bene on the right.

A problem position for Sebes was the holding role in midfield. He had players who could fill it, such as 1950s half-back József Zakariás, but no one who really stood out. On the other hand, there were plenty of more creative options such as Ernö Solymosi and, most especially, József Bozsik. Puskas lists right-half Bozsik as "the greatest player I ever saw or new". Such a testament was enough for Sebes, who'd make do without a midfield hard man.

Defenders

The defence looked pretty strong too. Kálmán Mészöly was one of the top centre-backs in the 1960s and was a sure thing for Sebes. Sweeper Sándor Matrai, a contemporary of Mészöly's, was chosen to partner him, although Laszlo Balint or big Gyular Lórant could also have done the job.

At right-back, Jenö Buzánszky added to the 1950s contingent, holding off challenges from Lajos Korányi from the 1938 side, and Sándor Sallai, a solid player in the 1980s.

József Varga was an attack minded left-back in the 1982 World Cup, but Sebes hardly needed more help going forward. He could have turned to the familiar Mihály Lantos for a physical presence, but instead went for Korányi's partner, Sándor Biró.

Goalkeepers

Gyula Grosics was chosen in goal. He won 82 caps between 1947 and 1962 and was one of the few 1950s stars not to flee Hungary after the October Uprising of 1956. Antal Szabó, a mainstay in the 1930s, would be the main back-up.

Hungary's strength was obviously in attack and if the defence could just keep things reasonable, Sebe's side looked like it might do some serious damage in a strong group.

Starting line-up (4-4-2)

Gyula Grosics; Jenö Buzánszky, Sándor Matrai, Kálmán Mészöly, Sándor Biró; Ferenc Bene, József Bozsik, Florian Albert, Zoltán Czibor; Ferenc Puskas, Sándor Kocsis

THE ALL-TIME WORLD CUP

HUNGARY WORLD CUP HISTORY

Year	Result	P	W	D	L
1930	Did not enter				
1934	Eliminated in quarter-finals	2	1	0	1
1938	Lost in Final	4	3	0	1
1950	Did not enter				
1954	Lost in Final	5	4	0	1
1958	Eliminated in round one	4	1	1	2
1962	Eliminated in quarter-finals	4	2	1	1
1966	Eliminated in quarter-finals	4	2	0	2
1970	Did not qualify				
1974	Did not qualify				
1978	Eliminated in round one	3	0	0	3
1982	Eliminated in round one	3	1	1	1
1986	Eliminated in round one	3	1	0	2
1990	Did not qualify				
1994	Did not qualify				
1998	Did not qualify				
Total		32	15	3	14

ITALY

Defence and more defence

Vittorio Pozzo was one of the truly great coaches of the pre-war years. A master tactician and the first coach to win the World Cup twice, Pozzo was an easy choice to head the Italian All-Time team.

Pozzo had possibly the largest talent pool to choose from. Italy's football history is both long and successful, and a number of great players have emerged through the years. A few of Pozzo's personal favourites were not available though. One of the first to poach South American stars for a national team, Pozzo prospered in the 1930s with the help of Luis Monti and Raimundo Orsi. They'd play for Argentina this time. Still, the cupboard was hardly bare.

44

THE CONTENDERS

Forwards

Up front, Silvio Piola was a certain starter. A Pozzo favourite, Piola was devastating in the 1930s, and Italy needed similar results this time. The battle to line up alongside Piola was intense. Paolo Rossi shot to fame with his six goals in 1982, but a short career counted against him. Luigi Riva was another sharp goalscorer and set an Italian record for most international goals, while the legends of Giampiero Boniperti and Valentino Mazzola (Sandro's father) were also hard to ignore. In the end, Pozzo chose a modern superstar in Roberto Baggio, who introduced himself with a marvellous goal in the 1990 World Cup and was one of the best two players in the tournament four years later.

Midfielders

In midfield, Pozzo opted for the dynamic Marco Tardelli on the right, which would allow Italy to switch effortlessly to 3-5-2 if they chose, with the left-back pushing on. To hold the midfield, Pozzo considered the tough Mario Bertini, but found an even better option. Romeo Benetti was brutal, but talented too - an irresistible combination for the Italians. With a mighty defensive wall in place, Pozzo could afford an extravagancy or two. Gianni Rivera fitted the bill. Highly skilled and beautiful to watch, Italy never quite figured out what to do with Rivera, but Pozzo had built him a platform and expected results. If he failed, his long-time rival - the technically gifted Sandro Mazzola - would step in. Giuseppe Meazza, the hub of Italy's wining sides in 1934 and 1938, completed the midfield, which meant no place for Giancarlo Antognoni, a smooth operator in the 1970s and early 1980s.

Defenders

Italian football has long been preoccupied with defence, a culture that has helped produce an incredible array of masterful defenders. The selection problems began at full-back. On the right Giuseppe Bergomi, an Inter Milan legend who won a World Cup as a teenager and remained on the International scene for another 16 years, was an obvious candidate. But he was by no means unopposed. Before Bergomi there was Tarcisio Burgnich, himself a veteran of three World Cups, and also the infamous Claudio Gentile, one of the most vicious man-markers, but also one of the best. Umberto Caligaris won 59 caps from 1922 to 1934 and was another strong candidate.

Italy have had just three full-time left-backs in the last 35 years. First came Giacinto Facchetti, who set the standard for attacking full-backs and formed a tremendous tandem with Burgnich. Tall, as good going forward as he was staying back, it was hard to imagine that he could be improved upon, but Italy

45

came close. Antonio Cabrini, who succeeded Facchetti, won a World Cup in 1982 and was one of the best defenders in the world. Then came Paolo Maldini. Arguably the greatest full-back of all-time, Maldini's combination of skill, pace and strength made him an awe-inspiring left-back, wing-back or centre-back. Pozzo was convinced and Maldini got the start.

At sweeper, Pozzo had to choose between the great Franco Baresi, or the man who kept him out of the Italian team for so many years, Gaeteno Scirea. Both had skills to go with the sharp edge, but Baresi's understanding with Maldini won the day. Having included three members of the 1990 Italian defence, Pozzo might have made it a full house. Riccardo Ferri was a fine man-marker and would have done well enough, but the competition was tough. Mauro Bellugi stood out in 1978, and Fulvio Collovati had been a key figure four years later. Another option was Luigi Allemandi, the left-back when Italy won the World Cup in 1934, but probably a centre-back in today's game. Collovati got the nod.

Bergomi, Baresi, Collovati and Maldini - it looked almost impregnable. The 1990 defence (with Ferri) kept five clean sheets on the way to the semi-finals and may be the greatest ever assembled, though the class of 1982 (Bergomi/Gentile, Collovati, Scirea, Cabrini) was pretty special too.

Goalkeepers

Dino Zoff, a veteran of three World Cups had the honour of defending the Italian goal. Walter Zenga, a star of Italia 1990, and Giampiero Combi, the 1934 skipper, acted as capable reserves.

Pozzo was confident he'd found the right balance. A strong backbone, fleshed out with some real flair and a few proven goal scorers. They might not be as exciting to watch as some, but they seemed certain to be there at the business end of the competition.

Starting line-up (4-2-2-2)

Dino Zoff; Giuseppe Bergomi, Franco Baresi, Fulvio Collovati, Paolo Maldini; Marco Tardelli, Romeo Benetti; Gianni Rivera, Giuseppe Meazza; Silvio Piola, Roberto Baggio

ITALY WORLD CUP HISTORY

Year	Result	P	W	D	L
1930	Did not enter				
1934	Champions	5	4	1	0
1938	Champions	4	4	0	0
1950	Eliminated in round one	2	1	0	1
1954	Eliminated in round one	3	1	0	2
1958	Did not qualify				
1962	Eliminated in round one	3	1	1	1
1966	Eliminated in round one	3	1	0	2
1970	Lost in Final	6	3	2	1
1974	Eliminated in round one	3	1	1	1
1978	Eliminated in round two (4th)	7	4	1	2
1982	Champions	7	4	3	0
1986	Eliminated in round two	4	1	2	1
1990	Eliminated in semi-finals	7	6	1*	0
1994	Lost in Final	7	4	2*	1
1998	Lost in quarter-finals	6	3	2*	1
Total		67	38	16	13

*Lost one game on penalties

SCOTLAND

The quest to progress

Given Scotland's less than impressive record in World Cup finals, finding a coach with a good international track record was a little tricky. By contrast, on the domestic scene several Scots have risen to the pinnacle of their profession. Bill Shankly, Matt Busby or Alex Ferguson may have sounded good enough to some, but Jock Stein had greater experience (not all of it good) on the international scene.

In almost every decade of the last century Scotland produced teams with one or two stars. Take those stand-outs, put them in one unit and, hey presto, you'd have a world-beater - or so Stein hoped.

Forwards

Denis Law would be the team's focal point. A European Footballer of the Year, a European Cup winner, and a player with a fine international scoring record, Law's credentials matched up with the very best. He only played in one World Cup finals however, late in his career in 1974, but hopes were high that he'd rise to this occasion.

The obvious choice to partner "The Lawman" was Kenny Dalglish, the Liverpool legend who played 102 times for his country and scored 30 goals. There were those who doubted Dalglish, however. In three World Cup finals tournaments he rarely delivered and Scotland couldn't afford a repeat of the let-downs. They had other options. Hughie Gallacher, for example, the supreme British centre-forward of the 1920s had the pedigree, even if he was somewhat untested at the highest level. Others in contention included Gallacher's rival Jimmy McGrory and post-war heroes like Lawrie Reilly and Billy Steel. Although he'd dropped Dalglish during the 1982 World Cup, Stein couldn't help but feel that his team needed the best player from the best team in Europe during the early 1980s. Law and Dalgish it was.

Midfielders

The midfield posed tactical as well as personnel problems. Should Stein use two flying wingers, or opt for greater numbers inside? He had plenty of alternatives, whichever route he chose. Graeme Souness was a good place to start. Strong and aggressive, but a playmaker too, the Liverpool midfielder looked tailor-made for the holding job. Stein picked him and hoped that his World Cup form would be better than on previous occasions. Of the attacking midfielders, Alex James had the best pedigree. A key figure in Herbert Chapman's dominant Arsenal sides, James was one of the first midfield generals. He had little international experience, having only won eight caps, but they included that impressive triumph at Wembley in 1928 when Scotland won 5-1 and were crowned the "Wembley Wizards". Battling James for a place was Jim Baxter. An enigmatic genius in the 1960s, Baxter also humiliated England on their own patch (in 1967) but was another without World Cup finals experience. Billy Bremner was chosen to back up Souness and Stein could start them as a pair if blood and guts was the order of the day.

The Scottish wing squadron was impressive. Billy Liddell, another Liverpool folk hero, little Willy Henderson, and the famous "Wizard" Alex Jackson were all viable choices. The first picks, however, were "jinkin" Jimmy Johnstone and Alan Morton, a 1920s hero. Stein would pick and mix on a match-by-match basis, but the ingredients were decent enough.

Denis Law

The Old Trafford faithful called him "The King" and many loved Denis Law even more than his famous partners Charlton and Best. An excellent all-round player, and magnificent marksman, Law is undoubtedly Scotland's greatest-ever player.

It's a little surprising that the Scots didn't reach a World Cup finals tournament during the sixties. Stars like Jim Baxter, Ian St John, Billy Bremner and Billy McNeil ought to have made them a real threat, but a play-off defeat against eventual runners-up Czechoslovakia in 1962 was the closest they came. The failures of the national team could hardly be blamed on Law, who scored an impressive 30 goals in 55 matches for his country. In 1974, Law played in his one and only finals match and was largely a bystander in a 2-0 win over Zaire.

If his Scotland story was shrouded in disappointment, Law's club career was full of triumph. He joined Huddersfield Town (where Bill Shankly was manager) in 1955 and made his league debut at the age of 16. He was still with Huddersfield when he scored on his Scotland debut but soon departed for Manchester City. After just one season at Maine Road he was sold to the Italian club Torino for £100,000. Law was unhappy with Torino, which he described as "like a prison", and after 10 goals in 27 games he packed his bags. Torino threatened legal action but eventually sanctioned a transfer to Manchester United where the trophies soon began to mount.

United won league titles, in 1963-64 and 1966-67, as well as the FA Cup in 1963. Law was particularly potent in that competition, netting 34 times in 44 games. Sharp reflexes in front of goal, as well as a prestigious leap that made him an aerial threat, helped Law score 171 goals in 305 League games for United. But it was in European competition that he was most deadly. He scored 28 times in 33 matches, but injury forced him out of the 1968 European Cup Final - United's greatest triumph.

As injury began to slow him, Law was granted a free transfer back to Manchester City in 1973. Under a year later he scored against United with a back-heel, a goal that helped doom United to relegation from the First Division. Old Trafford's favourite son did not celebrate, but walked solemnly back to the centre circle.

Law had a fiery temperament which often landed him in trouble with referees, but to the fans, and aficionados alike, Law will always be remembered as the greatest striker produced in the British Isles.

Defenders

In defence, Stein faced the same quandary - should Scotland take a gamble on domestic superstars with questionable international records? Dave McKay and Alan Hansen sounded pretty good as a central defensive pairing when thought of as a Tottenham double winner and Liverpool European champion, but where were the international credentials? George Young, long-time Scotland anchor at either right-back or centre-half, was a safer option and his strength matched well with Hansen's pace and poise. Billy McNeil and Richard Gough stood by.

At right-back, Danny McGrain was unopposed. A hard, but adventurous, Celtic player, McGrain was among the world's best in the 1970s. Steve Nicol acted as reserve. The left-back position was between Tommy Gemmell and Eric Caldow. The latter's greater consistency gave him the edge.

Goalkeepers

If the quality of the left-backs concerned Stein slightly, the goalkeeping spot must have given him nightmares. Famed for blunders, Scottish goalkeepers have an unenviable reputation. Even the best of them had their dodgy moments. Yashin, Banks, Maier...Leighton - something didn't quite fit. In fairness Scotland's number ones have improved over the years and so Stein went for the most recent regular custodian, Andy Goram. Leighton and Bill Brown would have to suffice as subs.

Altogether Stein had reason to be cheerful, but there'd be no repeat of Ally McLeod's 1978 declarations of intent. A win or two would do just fine.

Starting line-up (4-4-2)
Andy Goram; Danny McGrain, George Young, Alan Hansen, Eric Caldow; Jimmy Jonhstone, Alex James, Graeme Souness, Alan Morton; Kenny Dalglish, Denis Law

SCOTLAND WORLD CUP HISTORY

Year	Result	P	W	D	L
1930	Did not enter				
1934	Did not enter				
1938	Did not enter				
1950	Withdrew before finals				
1954	Eliminated in round one	2	0	0	2

1958	Eliminated in round one	3	0	1	2
1962	Did not qualify				
1966	Did not qualify				
1970	Did not qualify				
1974	Eliminated in round one	3	1	2	0
1978	Eliminated in round one	3	1	1	1
1982	Eliminated in round one	3	1	1	1
1986	Eliminated in round one	3	0	1	2
1990	Eliminated in round one	3	1	0	2
1994	Did not qualify				
1998	Eliminated in round one	3	0	1	2
Total		**23**	**4**	**7**	**12**

URUGUAY

Champions remembered

In recent times Uruguay's national team has struggled to make an impact, failing to qualify for the World Cup in either 1994 or 1998. For many years, however, before the rise of Brazil, Uruguay were the world's dominant footballing nation.

Juan López isn't a household name in Europe but he should be. It was he who led his team to a surprise World Cup win in 1950 and was in charge again four years later. He carried Uruguay's hopes here.

Several legends from the 1950s, and from the dominant side of the 1920s and 1930s, were rolled out in the hope of reviving a long-forgotten winning instinct.

Forwards
The history lesson began with Oscar Omar Míguez, the eccentric star of Peñarol and centre-forward when Uruguay lifted the World Cup in 1950. Many Uruguayan experts rate Míguez as their greatest ever striker. Fernando Morena, another contender for that title, is the most successful goal scorer ever in Uruguayan club football. Morena was unfortunate to arrive on the international scene as Uruguay's team fell into decline in the 1970s. Nonetheless, he managed to bag 22 goals while winning 54 caps. Walter Gómez, a River Plate legend, who was kept out of the 1950 side by Míguez, and 1920s mainstay Pedro Petrone were the other contenders, but López chose the familiar Míguez as a

51

lone striker with two wide players in support.

This has been the Uruguay way ever since 1950, when they introduced an early version of 4-3-3. The two full-backs moved into the centre, with the wing-halves covering the flanks. The centre-half took command of the midfield, assisted by the inside forwards, with the centre-forward and wingers pushed forward.

Lopez's problem in sticking with this formation, however, was that Uruguay has never produced a world-class left-wing, with the possible exception of Pablo Dorado. On the right - by contrast - the options were plentiful, with López able to choose between little Alcide Ghiggia, who scored the winner against Brazil in 1950, and Luis Cubilla of 1970s fame.

Attacking midfielders were also in plentiful supply. Uruguay's favoured system has produced a host of skilled playmakers who prospered in what we today call "the hole".

The most famous of these - and Uruguay's greatest player - is Juan Schiaffino, who stood out in 1950 and again in 1954. In 1958 he led AC Milan to the European Cup Final. López decided that Schiaffino could push up to support Míguez and Cubilla.

Midfielders

Behind the forward line Uruguay fielded two World Cup legends. José Leandro Andrade was the first black star of international football, right-half and physical dominator for Uruguay from 1923-1930. Although Andrade could have been slotted in at right-back, López decided to partner him with Obdulio Varela, the World Cup captain in 1950. An attacking centre-half, Varela had a midfield role, dominating from end to end but could also drop back to do more defensive duties if necessary. Together Andrade and Varela would form a formidable barrier in midfield.

To complete the midfield, Uruguay had the choice of several fine play-makers. Hector Scarone is Uruguay's all-time top goal scorer. Starting as a striker he became the schemer who ran the show during the first World Cup, and seemed a must for this side. His inclusion posed a problem however. The side was heavily loaded towards the right flank, and Scarone was an inside-right. Pedro Rocha offered a little balance. Another fine midfield general, he operated from the inside-left position in the 1960s and this swayed López.

The selection also left no room for Néstor Goncalvez, an icon in the 1960s, and Enzo Francescoli, the Uruguayan version of Diego Maradona in the 1980s. Scarone, Goncalvez and Francescoli - not bad for the bench.

Defenders

Uruguayan football has been known for its attention to defence since the very early days, so López had plenty of choice at the back. At right-back, Andrade's nephew Victor Rodríguez Andrade was a shoe-in. Right-half in the early 50s, Rodríguez's provided a combination of skill and strength and would link with his uncle down the right. The left side was again more difficult. Shubert Gambetta was Rodríguez's wing-half partner in 1950 and a national team regular for a decade, and so had the pedigree, but so did Alvaro Gestido, left-half in 1930. Both would have been safe enough but López wanted to add a touch of the modern and went for Alfonso Pereyra. A left-winger as well as left-back in the late 1970s, Pereyra would give the team much needed width down the flank.

José Nasazzi, captain of Uruguay's first great team, was chosen to anchor the defence. He was nominally a right-back, but generally played in the centre, often behind his fellow defenders and so would fit in well in the middle. There were many possible partners for Nasazzi, starting with the central defensive pairing of 1954, José Santamaría and Willam Martínez. Santamaría went on to play a key part in Real Madrid's early European success, while Martínez retired as his country's most capped player. The choice didn't end there. Matthias Gonzalez was the top defender in 1950, one whom Varela called "an incredible player", while Roberto Matosas and Attilio Ancheta were excellent as Uruguay progressed to the World Cup semi-finals in 1970.

Goalkeepers

López had three great goalkeeping options. Ladislao Mazurkiewicz, who was exceptional in the 1970s, got the start, but 1950s regular Roque Máspoli and Andrés Mazali, from the 1920s, were world class and unlucky to have to sit on the sidelines.

It required a good memory - and a long life - to fully appreciate this Uruguayan side, but there was no mistaking the quality.

Starting line-up (5-2-3)

Ladislao Mazurkiewicz; Victor Rodríguez Andrade, José Santamaría, José Nasazzi, Obdulio Varela, Alfonso Pereyra; José Leandro Andrade, Pedro Rocha; Luis Cubilla, Oscar Omar Míguez, Juan Schiaffino

URUGUAY WORLD CUP HISTORY

Year	Result	P	W	D	L
1930	Champions	4	4	0	0
1934	Did not enter				
1938	Did not enter				
1950	Champions	4	3	1	0
1954	Eliminated in semi-finals	5	3	0	2
1958	Did not qualify				
1962	Eliminated in round one	3	1	0	2
1966	Eliminated in quarter-finals	4	1	2	1
1970	Eliminated in semi-finals (4th)	6	2	1	3
1974	Eliminated in round one	3	0	1	2
1978	Did not qualify				
1982	Did not qualify				
1986	Eliminated in round two	4	0	2	2
1990	Eliminated in round two	4	1	1	2
1994	Did not qualify				
1998	Did not qualify				
Total		**37**	**15**	**8**	**14**

ARGENTINA

Talent to burn

In 1978, Argentina, the last of great football powers not to have won the World Cup, staged the competition. There was great pressure on the team, especially the coach. Cesar Menotti duly delivered the trophy and was therefore a justified choice to lead the All-Time Argentina side. Carlos Bilardo, World Cup winner in 1986, and even Juan Carlos Lorenzo had some support, but their pragmatic and sometimes brutal tactics didn't sit well with the spirit of this competition.

Forwards

With a midfield like theirs, Argentina's strikers would only have to stay upright to score goals. Gabriel Batistuta and Mario Kempes could stand just fine, and scored a goal or two as well. Batistuta's prolific spell in Italy, as well as over 50 goals for his country, and Kempes's six-goal heroics in 1978, gave them the edge on the starting places, but there was stiff opposition. Juan Manuel Moreno, for instance, has a following that still claims him to be Argentina's finest ever player. He played inside-right in the famed "Maquina" River Plate forward line of the 1940s. His partners in crime, Angel Labruna and Adolfo Pedernera, were also contenders. The prolific Luis Artime and 1970s stars René Houseman and attacking midfielder Carlos Babington were left on the fringes.

Midfield

Luis Monti played for Argentina in the Olympic Final of 1928 and the 1930 World Cup Final. He then moved to Italy and won the trophy with his adopted country in 1934. Although often referred to as an attacking centre-half, Monti was more of a midfield ball winner who would crunch his opponents and then spread long passes to his wingers. Although Argentina has produced a whole stream of successors to Monti, including Nestor Rossi, the infamous Antonio Rattin, and recently Fernando Redondo, Menotti decided that the original was still the best.

With such a pillar in place Argentina could afford to splurge on some extravagant skill. They didn't come much better than Diego Maradona. Small but strong, as well as quick, Maradona's dynamic skill almost single-handedly won the World Cup in 1986. Menotti, who'd left a 17-year old Maradona out of his 1978 squad, just had to figure out where to play him. Although sometimes a centre-forward, Maradona's play-making skills were best suited to a deeper position. In this team Diego would roam free, but would nominally start on the left. Inside him would be Alfredo Di Stefano, who vies with Maradona as the greatest ever Argentine-born player. Like Monti, Di Stefano also made his name abroad - in Spain with Real Madrid - but started his career in his native Argentina, which welcomed him back with open arms. Although listed as a centre-forward, Di Stefano was another who preferred to spend his time in midfield, dictating play as well as scoring goals. Osvaldo Ardiles, a Menotti favourite from 1978, was chosen to complete the midfield and would play on the right. Ardiles, Monti, Di Stefano and Maradona - it looked unstoppable. The reserves were decent too. Raimundo Orsi, another Argentine-turned-Italian, covered on the left, while Rattin would back up Monti. Other excellent squad players included Juventus great Omar Sivori, Manchester United's import Juan-Sebastian Veron, Jorge Burruchaga and Miguel Brindisi.

Defenders

Daniel Passarella would lead the side from his customary sweeper position. Strong and forceful, Passarella captained Argentina's first World Cup winners and hoped to repeat the trick. Alongside him would be Oscar Ruggeri, who won

97 caps in 11 years from 1983. He narrowly held off the challenges of Roberto Perfumo, a stalwart in 1966 and 1974, and Passarella's 1978 partner Luis Galván, as well as another 1970s star Osvaldo Piazza.

Silvio Marzolini isn't particularly famous in Europe, which is a great shame. One of the first - and best - attacking left-backs, he'd aim to conquer some excellent Group Four right-wingers. Alberto Tarantini was chosen as back up on the left, while his 1978 partner, Jorge Olguin, was chosen to start on the right ahead of the flying Javier Zanetti.

Goalkeepers
Ubaldo Fillol was a steadying influence on Menotti's triumphant side in the 1970s, and the obvious choice here. Amedeo Carrizo had a long and distinguished career, although his part in the 6-1 defeat at the hands of Czechoslovakia in the 1958 World Cup counted against him.

Menotti appeared to have all the tools to take the Cup back to Argentina. The spine of Fillol, Passarella, Monti and Batistuta was pretty special and no team had a one-two punch like Maradona and Di Stefano.

Starting line-up (4-1-3-2)
Ubaldo Fillol; Jorge Olguin, Daniel Passarella, Oscar Ruggeri, Silvio Marzolini; Luis Monti; Osvaldo Ardiles, Alfredo Di Stefano, Diego Maradona; Mario Kempes, Gabriel Batistuta

ARGENTINA WORLD CUP HISTORY

Year	Result	P	W	D	L
1930	Lost in Final	5	4	0	1
1934	Eliminated in round one	1	0	0	1
1938	Did not enter				
1950	Did not enter				
1954	Did not enter				
1958	Eliminated in round one	3	1	0	2
1962	Eliminated in round one	3	1	1	1
1966	Eliminated in quarter-finals	4	1	1	2
1970	Did not qualify				
1974	Eliminated in round two	6	1	2	3
1978	Champions	7	5	1	1
1982	Eliminated in round two	5	2	0	3
1986	Champions	7	6	1	0

1990	Lost in Final	7	3	2*	2
1994	Eliminated in round two	4	2	0	2
1998	Eliminated in quarter-finals	5	3	1*	1
Total		**57**	**29**	**9**	**19**

*Won one game on penalties

HOLLAND

Totally Talented

It's not entirely clear who invented the term "Total Football". It was first used to describe the 1974 Dutch side, but the style was developed at Ajax during the late 1960s. Some say that the players - and in particular Johan Cruyff - were the innovators, but most commonly Rinus Michels is given the lion's share of the credit. Michels became coach of Ajax in 1965 and together with Cryuff transformed them into the greatest side in Europe. The emphasis was on attack, not just by the forwards, but by everyone. Defence wasn't neglected, however. If the right-back attacked, the right midfielder would drop back, and so on. Every player attacks, every player defends. Simple, but revolutionary. Michels went on to lead Holland to the World Cup Final in 1974, and re-emerged as coach of Holland in the 1988 European Championships. No one else was considered for the All-Time job.

Forwards

For Michels, for Holland, it all begins with Cruyff. Intelligent, quick and skilled, he simply had it all. A luxury player who worked hard; a gifted natural who thought scientifically. No praise is too high. Cruyff flitted between attack and midfield, from the centre to the wings. Supposedly a centre-forward, he was often found turning opponents out wide. Michels listed him on the left for this team but knew what to expect.

Late in his career Cruyff served as mentor to Marco van Basten, who developed into one of the most complete centre-forwards. Tall, athletic and deadly in front of goal, he emulated Cruyff in becoming a three-times European Footballer of the Year.

Van Basten's partner in the magnificent side of 1988, and at AC Milan, was Ruud Gullit. Another intelligent all-rounder, Gullit played as a striker, a midfielder, a winger and sweeper. Strong, good in air and sublime on the deck, he'd play to the right of Van Basten and Cruyff in an exceptional forward line.

57

The quality of the front three left no room for some other fine footballers. Many of those who coached or played with Rob Rensenbrink rate him alongside Cruyff, although he was often overshadowed by his more extrovert team mate. A great dribbler and passer, Rensenbrink was often required to play on the wing for Holland to make room for Cruyff, but in Belgium, where he starred for Anderlecht and Brugge, he roamed through the middle and looked one of the best players in the world.

Brilliant wingers Piet Keizer, Coen Moulijn and Marc Overmars all deserved a look, but no-one was about to oust Cruyff or Gullit. Dennis Bergkamp came closer to challenging Van Basten. He shone for Ajax, Arsenal and Holland in the 1990s, but unlike his predecessor had not impressed in Italy. The likes of Johnny Rep, Patrick Kluivert and Faas Wilkes were worthy of consideration, but never stood a chance. Wilkes' team mate Abe Lenstra was another left on the sidelines, a sign of Holland's progress in recent years. Until Cruyff, Lenstra was regarded as his country's greatest ever player.

Midfield

There are those that believe Johan Neeskens was as important to Ajax and Holland in the 1970s as Cruyff. Neeskens provided the power and aggression that allowed his gifted team mates to work their magic. He chased down and intimidated opponents, but could score and create too. As one-time team mate Sjaak Swart put it: "Neeskens could play for two."

One of those who made use of the ball that Neeskens won was Wim van Hanegem, the midfield playmaker. If the Dutch national team was better than Ajax, it was only because it called on the inspiration of Feyenoord.

Edgar Davids completed the midfield, providing incredible energy and speed that galvanized some very good Juventus sides in the late 1990s. Given the presence of Neeskens, and the fact that Van Hanegem could also put his foot in, it was arguable that Michels didn't need a another ball winner, but it wasn't as if the Dutch were short of flair either.

Holland's 1934 World Cup captain Puck van Heel and the versatile Ronald de Boer, were among those to miss out.

Defenders

The legacy of Total Football is that Holland's finest defenders are also great going forward. Full-backs Wim Suurbier and Ruud Krol rarely met an opponent they couldn't handle in the 1970s, but could also move forward, adding to the team's attacking menace. Neither had a serious rival for a place in this team, although Michael Reiziger has been one of the best right-backs in the world for the last five years.

If the 1974 side had a comparative weakness it was in central defence. The team missed the presence of Ajax stopper Barry Hulshoff, although Arie Haan, a fine midfielder, and Wim Rijsbergen, who moved over from full-back, did well as stop-gaps. Luckily for Michels, the 1988 side featured the brilliant partnership of Ronald Koeman and Frank Rijkaard. The blonde Koeman was slow and sometimes looked ponderous, but he read the game well and launched many attacks from his sweeper spot.

Rijkaard was perhaps even better as a midfielder for AC Milan, but for Holland he played the role of defender - and played it pretty damn well. Frank de Boer is Holland's most capped player, and has been one of the best European central defenders in recent years. He'd allow Michels to move Rijkaard further forward if necessary.

Goalkeepers

Injury and his poor relationship with Cruyff meant that Jan van Beveren didn't feature in a World Cup, but he's commonly regarded as the country's best Number One. Edwin van der Sar began to challenge that idea in the 1990s with some outstanding displays and would step in if Van Beveren's form deserted him. One-time Nottingham Forrest keeper and 1988 custodian Hans van Breukelen went along for the ride.

Style, skill, strength and speed - what was missing from Michel's side? Unity was the only concern as the Dutch have been famous for damaging internal disputes. With personalities such as Cruyff, Gullit and Rijkaard all gathered in one squad, sparks were liable to fly again. Michels hoped to keep the fireworks on the pitch.

Starting line-up (4-3-3)
Jan van Beveren; Wim Suurbier, Ronald Koeman, Frank Rijkaard, Ruud Krol; Edgar Davids, Johan Neeskens, Wim van Hanegem; Ruud Gullit, Marco van Basten, Johan Cruyff

59

THE ALL-TIME WORLD CUP

HOLLAND WORLD CUP HISTORY

Year	Result	P	W	D	L
1930	Did not enter				
1934	Eliminated in round one	1	0	0	1
1938	Eliminated in round one	1	0	0	1
1950	Did not qualify				
1954	Did not qualify				
1958	Did not qualify				
1962	Did not qualify				
1966	Did not qualify				
1970	Did not qualify				
1974	Lost in Final	7	5	1	1
1978	Lost in Final	7	3	2	2
1982	Did not qualify				
1986	Did not qualify				
1990	Eliminated in round two	4	0	3	1
1994	Eliminated in quarter-finals	5	3	0	2
1998	Eliminated in semi-finals (4th)	7	3	3*	1
Total		**31**	**14**	**9**	**9**

*Lost one game on penalties

PORTUGAL

Better than their record

Brazilian Otto Glória was coach when Portugal produced their best World Cup finish - third in 1966 - and was a narrow choice to lead this side, ahead of Humberto Coelho who guided Portugal to the semi-finals of the European Championships in 2000.

With Glória in charge, and given the player resources at his disposal, an attacking and exciting line-up was assured.

Forwards

They didn't come much more attacking or exciting than Eusebio. Top scorer in 1966, European Footballer of the Year the previous season, he wasn't called the European Pelé for nothing.

Alongside him Glória chose Eusebio's national team and Benfica partner José Torres, a giant centre-forward who'd proven virtually impossible to stop in the air. His predecessor - another African import - José Águas, was also in contention, but the 12 goals Eusebio and Torres scored between them in the World Cup in England persuaded the coach to leave well enough alone. Two stand-outs from the 1980s, Chalana and Nené, supplied further back-up.

Midfielders

If Eusebio is the universal choice as Portugal's greatest player, he now has a rival. Luis Figo's performances with Barcelona, Real Madrid, and especially Portugal, have elevated him to the very top of many experts' ranking of the world's best players. A right-sided midfielder blending surprising strength with beautiful skill, Figo would be Eusebio's main provider in this team.

Another goal creator was Mário Coluña, a stocky, Mozambique-born inside-forward whose great athleticism and long-range shooting made him a star with Benfica. Coluna's inclusion left little room for Rui Costa, Figo's able assistant in the 2000 side. A skilful playmaker, it was sad Portugal couldn't find him a starting berth, but he was sure to feature at some point.

The wingers in 1966 - Antônio Simôes and José Augusto - were options for this side too, but Figo blocked Augusto's path, while Simôes lost out to the famous Paulo Futre. Although he never quite seemed to fulfil his potential, in his youth Futre sparkled for FC Porto.

Paulo Sousa was entrusted with winning the forwards the ball. A successful player with Juventus, he formed a fearsome trio with Rui Costa and Figo for the national team.

Defenders

As with Aguas, the World Cup of 1966 came a little late for Germano, one of Europe's best stoppers in the early 1960s, and the steel in Benfica's European Cup-winning side. Humberto Coelho was a fine centre-half before he began coaching and was candidate to join Germano, but he eventually lost out to Fernando Couto. With his long flowing locks, Couto excelled in Italy in the 1990s and his ability to play sweeper or as an emergency midfielder made him invaluable.

Another player from the Portugal's successful 1990s side was Manuel Dimas, a solid full-back. He could switch to the right if needed, but he'd start on the left where there was little competition other than Toni, a decent full-back from the 1970s.

Portugal have successfully employed two players named João Pinto over the last 20 years. The first, João Domingos Silva Pinto, was an important component at right-back in the team that reached the European Championships of 1984. He went on to win 70 caps, a record which striker João Manuel Vieira Pinto was well on his way to matching in the run-up to the 2002 World Cup.

Goalkeepers

Alberto da Costa Pereira, Benfica's European Cup-winning goalie, was a strong candidate for the number one jersey, but there were others in the mix. Vitor Baia emerged as one of Europe's best in the 1990s, playing with Porto and Barcelona. Manuel Bento was a decent custodian in the 1980s and third choice for Glória's side.

For a supposed outsider, Portugal's line-up looked scarily strong. It was tempting to say they'd be vulnerable at the back, but Germano, Costa Pereira and Couto were no pushovers. A prolonged stay was still a long-shot, but certainly not impossible.

Starting line-up (4-4-2)

Alberto da Costa Pereira; João Domingos Silva Pinto, Fernando Couto, Germano, Dimas; Luis Figo, Paulo Sousa, Mário Coluña, Paulo Futre; Eusebio, José Torres

PORTUGAL WORLD CUP HISTORY

Year	Result	P	W	D	L
1930	Did not enter				
1934	Did not qualify				
1938	Did not qualify				
1950	Did not qualify				
1954	Did not qualify				
1958	Did not qualify				
1962	Did not qualify				
1966	Eliminated in semi-finals	6	5	0	1
1970	Did not qualify				
1974	Did not qualify				
1978	Did not qualify				
1982	Did not qualify				
1986	Eliminated in round one	3	1	0	2
1990	Did not qualify				
1994	Did not qualify				
1998	Did not qualify				
Total		**9**	**6**	**0**	**3**

Eusebio

They called him Europe's answer to Pelé, a tag that would have fitted nicely if Eusebio was actually from Europe. He was born in Mozambique and starred there for a nursery side of Sporting Clube de Portugal. However, on arrival in Portugal, it was Sporting's great rival Benfica that snagged the young striker, who made his debut in 1961.

Eusebio soon helped his new club to reach new heights. Benfica were Europe's new superpower, having deposed Real Madrid as European Champions, and with Eusebio on board soon became unstoppable. Benfica retained the Euopean Cup in 1962, with Eusebio scoring twice in a 5-3 thriller against Real. Over the next five seasons, Benfica reached three more European Cup Finals, but lost each time - the last to Manchester United in the famous 1968 clash.

On the domestic scene, Benfica remained the dominant force, winning 10 titles in Eusebio's 14 years with the club.

In 1965 Eusebio was named European Footballer of the Year and the following year was the leading scorer in the World Cup finals. The tournament in England marked the only appearance in the finals for Eusebio as Portugal failed to qualify in 1962 or 1970. But Eusebio certainly left his mark in 1966. He played a key role in Portugal's opening match, a win against fancied Hungary, before going on a goal-scoring tear. One against Bulgaria and two against Pelé's Brazil preceded four in a remarkable quarter-final win over North Korea. Portugal were 3-0 down before Eusebio went to work.

The striker scored his eighth in the semi-final loss to England, and rounded things off with the first goal in the third-place play-off. In total, Eusebio scored 41 goals in 64 games for his country.

Today the phrase "power and pace" is something of a cliché - but of all the players associated with those most useful of qualities, nobody embodied them better than Eusebio. He scored many goals running on to through balls, using his strength to hold off opponents, or his speed to outstrip them. Dribbling skills and a mighty shot rounded off his arsenal, which, even in the company of Pelé and George Best, counted as one of the most fearsome of his day.

RUSSIA

Weakened by the break-up

Like Portugal, the Soviet Union made its best World Cup showing in 1966, where they reached the semi-finals. The coach of that side, Nikolai Morozov, was selected to lead Russia in the All-Time tournament.

Morozov's job was a difficult one. The Soviet Union was a consistent second-tier power from the late 1950s until the country fell apart in the early 1990s, but many of those sides had relied heavily on players from the now independent Ukraine, Georgia and Lithuania.

Nonetheless, Russia had enough stars to make it through qualification, but they were desperately thin in some departments.

Forwards

The Soviet Union's most famous striker, Oleg Blokhin, heralded from Ukraine and so was unavailable to Morozov. Other Soviet stars - Protasov, Belanov and Simonian - were also on call elsewhere, which left the Russians a little short on choices. However, the two that they chose to start certainly had the pedigree. Eduard Streltsov is regarded by many observers of Soviet football as the finest ever Russian outfield player, and is sometimes even likened to Pelé. Talented on the ball and a sharp shooter, Streltsov won an Olympic gold medal in 1956 in what was probably the best of all Soviet sides.

Vsevolod Bobrov was the captain of the Soviet Union in the 1952 Olympics and he scored a hat-trick in a 5-5 draw with eventual winner Yugloslavia. Neither Streltsov or Bobrov played in a World Cup as the Soviet Union didn't enter their first tournament until 1958. Anatoly Ilyin, who scored the winning goal in the 1956 Olympic Final, was chosen as the first reserve.

Midfielders

Soviet greats Valentin Ivanov and Igor Netto would form the basis of the midfield. Netto was a smooth operator at left-half who made the play, but could put his weight about too (most Soviet teams were physically imposing). Ivanov was a brilliant inside-forward, capable of beating men on the dribble and scoring spectacular goals. He was the outstanding player of the 1960 European Nations Cup and a key factor in the successful Soviet sides of the late 1950s and early 1960s. Valery Voronin was Netto's wing-half partner in the 1962 World Cup and also played in 1966. Another fine passer, Voronin also helped marshal the defence.

Also of 1960s vintage was Igor Chislenko, a tiny but excellent right-winger who was particularly outstanding in the 1966 World Cup. Indeed, his injury in the semi-final with Germany was a critical factor in the Soviet Union's defeat. Chislenko would be covered by Andrei Kanchelskis, a Ukrainian who starred for Manchester United and chose to represent Russia after the break-up of the Soviet Union.

Valeri Karpin, one of the best players to represent Russia since it's independence, hoped to dislodge Netto or Voronin, as would 1980s star Fyodor Cherenkov.

Defenders

For many years, the Soviet Union's defence was one of the most feared in the world. Playing in front of the likes of Yashin and Dasayev certainly helped but there were great defenders too. Albert Schesternev heads the list. Schesternev led the Soviets in 1966 and was equally capable as a sweeper or as a traditional stopper centre-half. Strong, and intimidating, he was also useful on the ball and surprising sprightly for such a huge man.

Unfortunately, several other fine defenders were claimed by Ukraine or Georgia. Still, 1980s sweeper Vagiz Khidiatulin was decent enough, as was Dmitri Khlestov, a recent star with Spartak Moscow and Turkey's Besiktas. Victor Onopko is perhaps the best player to represent Russia since the dissolution of the Soviet Union. Onopko has played for the Soviet Union, the interim Commonwealth of Independent States and Russia. A sweeper, and sometimes a midfielder, Onopko started as a left-sided defender, where he would operate for Morozov's team.

Goalkeepers

One area where Russia boasted both quality and depth was in goal. There hasn't been a better goalkeeper than Lev Yashin, the man in black. It's no surprise that he was on hand when the Soviet Union did well in England, or when they made the first two European Championship Finals.

In 1988, the Soviets again reached the European Championship Final, inspired to a great extent by Renat Dasayev, who lost little in comparison with his famous predecessor. He starred in two World Cups.

Lev Yashin

In England, many argue that Gordon Banks is greatest of all goalkeepers, but the rest of the world is well aware that the title belongs to Russia's Lev Yashin. Yashin was the talisman of the national team when the Soviet Union emerged on to the World football scene in the 1950s. To the West, Yashin,

dressed in all back, seemed to epitomise the Soviet threat. Big, dominant, perhaps even unbeatable.

After finally choosing football over ice hockey, Yashin made his national team debut in 1954 and two years later kept a clean sheet in the Olympic Final as the Soviets defeated Yugoslavia. Entering the 1958 World Cup, the Soviets were seen by many as favourites. With players like Yashin, Valantin Ivanov and Nikita Simonian, it was easy to see why. In the event, having beaten England in a play-off to qualify for the quarter-finals, they lost to the hosts Sweden, who went on to reach the final.

Yashin and his team were back four years later, and looked even better having added the likes of Igors, Netto and Chislenko, to the mix. Again they reached the quarter-finals, again going down to the hosts - Chile.

In 1966, two clean-sheets from Yashin helped the Soviets advance to the quarter-finals for a third time, and this time they were successful, beating Hungary 2-1. They later lost the semi-final with West Germany when Yashin strangely didn't respond to Beckenbauer's winning shot.

Yashin played his last match for the national team in 1967, although he was again in the Soviet squad for the 1970 World Cup.

Yashin had even greater success in the European Championship, which the Soviet Union won in 1960 (it was called the "European Nations Cup" back then). They were able to do so in large part due to their goalkeeper, who kept his side in the Final with a series of saves as they faced an onslaught from Yugoslavia in the first half. In 1964, Yashin was again the tournament's star. He held Italy at bay almost single-handedly in the second round - even saving a penalty - before playing a crucial role in the quarter-final victory over Sweden. The Soviets eventually fell in the Final to the hosts Spain, despite another inspired Yashin display.

Strangely for a country of its size, and for one with such a strong sporting heritage, Russia has only ever produced one footballer that ranks with the game's greats.

But if you're only going to have one standard-bearer, Lev Yashin is a pretty safe pair of hands.

There wasn't too much depth in this Russian team, a consequence of losing so many fine players from the other Soviet Republics, but at least Morozov could call on one or two genuine world-beaters. Soviet sides were often expected to do well in World Cups and invariably shone in the group stages before fading away. This time there were no grand expectations - if Russia managed to escape from a tough group, it would be a major surprise.

Starting line-up (1-3-3-3)
Lev Yashin; Vagiz Khidiatulin; Dmitri Khlestov, Albert Schesternev, Victor Onopko; Valery Voronin, Valentin Ivanov, Igor Netto; Igor Chislenko, Eduard Streltsov, Vsevolod Bobrov

RUSSIA WORLD CUP HISTORY

Year	Result	P	W	D	L
1930	Did not enter				
1934	Did not enter				
1938	Did not enter				
1950	Did not enter				
1954	Did not enter				

1958	Eliminated in quarter-finals	5	2	1	2
1962	Eliminated in quarter-finals	4	2	1	1
1966	Eliminated in semi-finals (4th)	6	4	0	2
1970	Eliminated in quarter-finals	4	2	1	1
1974	Did not qualify				
1978	Did not qualify				
1982	Eliminated in round two	5	2	2	1
1986	Eliminated in round two	4	2	1	1
1990	Eliminated in round one	3	1	0	2
1994	Eliminated in round one	3	1	0	2
1998	Did not enter				
Total		**34**	**16**	**6**	**12**

Russia participated as part of the Soviet Union 1958-1990

THE MATCHES

GROUP ONE:
Brazil, England, Rep. of Ireland, Sweden

The first group re-ignited a few old World Cup rivalries. Brazil were the group's 800lb gorilla, four-times World Cup winners, and a contender in every tournament since 1938. Sweden were particularly unhappy to see the South Americans, having met them on seven occasions in five different World Cups. Two draws and five losses didn't bode too well, although the games had gotten progressively closer. The first meeting, in the 1938 Final Pool, saw Leônidas and company hand out a 7-1 thrashing, and Pelé scored twice in the 1958 Final in which the Swedes were dismissed 5-2. Since then, no match has been decided by more than a single goal, including the 1994 semi-final which saw Romario score the winner. With both teams drawing heavily from their 1958 squads, there would be a few reunions, which presumably suited Brazil just fine.

England have their history with Brazil as well, and haven't fared any better. Three World Cup meetings, yielding just one draw - the first ever 0-0 game in the World Cup finals, in 1958. That marked England's high point against Brazil in the World Cup, especially as they'd lost several key players (Duncan Edwards, Roger Byrne and Tommy Taylor) to the Munich air crash earlier that year. In 1956, England had actually beaten Brazil at Wembley. In the years since, England have received a 3-1 football lesson in 1962 and lost the epic 1970 first round duel. Widely regarded as one of the best World Cup matches of all, Jairzinho scored the only goal in a match-up between the two best teams in the tournament - or at least that's what the English called it.

England have avoided Brazil since then, partly because they've failed to qualify for three of the seven subsequent finals tournaments. The Brazil-England match was expected to decide the group and would bring the game's founders face to face with its spiritual guardians. Bobby Moore would get to dance with Pelé once more, and Wilson hoped to do better against Garrincha.

Ireland's recent record against England has also been quite impressive. In the World Cup, they have met only once - in 1990 - when two well-organised teams fought out a 0-0 draw. Of the players ready to face up in Group One, the likes of Lineker, Robson, McGrath and Aldridge had played that day.

England and Sweden tangled in the qualifiers for "Italia 90", but have not met in the finals (prior to 2002). The two countries do share some strong ties, however. Both share a similar, physical style of play, and each has provided the other with an accomplished coach. England will hope that Sven-Goran Eriksson's appointment as England coach in the run-up to the World Cup in Japan and Korea brings as much success as Sweden saw under George Raynor's stewardship in the 1940s and 1950s.

Sweden and Ireland have no World Cup finals history but both were aware that to stand a chance in this tough group they'd need to beat the rival minnow. Ireland have also avoided the might of Brazil and, like everyone else, would have preferred to have done so again.

Statistically this was a fairly strong group. Between them, the four teams won five World Cups, lost in the Final three times and made the semi-final stage on seven occasions, the best collective record of any group in the tournament.

ENGLAND 1 REP. IRELAND 1

It was only fitting that England should be involved in the tournament's opening game, although Ireland, and not Scotland were the opponents. In many ways Ireland has become the "new enemy" after a number of intense matches. This encounter was no different, and the Irish once again played above themselves to cast serious doubts over England's credentials.

Ireland got off to the best possible start, scoring after just 10 minutes. For England fans it brought back several old horrors. Once again it seemed that a side much fancied on paper would be found wanting on the grass. But England have never lacked for bravery and determination and - eventually - they played themselves back into the game and the tournament.

Ireland's opener was typical of a Charlton team. Frank Stapleton challenged Bobby Moore for a high ball that the England skipper only partially cleared, Roy Keane drilled it back into the box and after a ricochet, it fell to John Aldridge who poked it home.

England's confidence was rocked and the Irish remained in the ascendancy for the next half an hour. For all the talk of long ball, Ireland possessed some fine footballers. Brady - enjoying the support of Keane and Giles - prompted and probed as the Irish remained a menace.

England were struggling badly in midfield where Edwards was a lone warrior. Bobby Charlton, Stanley Matthews and Finney were fine players, but not diligent defenders and Ireland simply out-hustled them. One passage of play illustrated the problem. England stroked the ball neatly around midfield as Keane chased and harried. Eventually a pass went astray, Giles nipped in and started another attack. Once Ireland had the ball, there was precious little pressure applied by England's midfield.

Ramsey had seen enough and, after the break, made a change. Finney, well marked by Carey, and again below par at World Cup level, was removed and Bryan Robson was introduced in the middle. Bobby Charlton moved out to the left. The impact was almost immediate. Robson introduced himself to Brady with a brutal but fair challenge, Edwards picked up the loose ball, moved past Giles and Keane then knocked it to Charlton on the left. The balding maestro stepped inside Carey and thrashed a right-footed rocket high into the Bonner's goal. A great player, doing what he did best when it was needed most.

After that it was all England, finally looking like a former World Champion. Edwards and Robson imposed their considerable will over the midfield, which seemed to galvanise the rest of the side. Matthews, quiet until now, started to attack Irwin, one of the most successful players in the English game but highlighted by Ramsey as a possible weak link. Three times the grand old man of English football skinned his opponent. The first cross was glanced just wide by Lineker. Greaves completely missed Matthews' second attempt, before connecting well with the third. Bonner was equal to it, but only just.

Ramsey brought on Keegan near the end in the hope that an extra implosion of energy would push England over the top. He came close with a stooping header, but it was just wide. Shades of 1982 all over again.

A disappointing result for England, but not the disaster it might have seemed. Ramsey had come closer to discovering his best team, one that played to England's (physical?) strengths.

Ireland had looked good in patches, mixing strength and skill, but they'd been over-run once Robson entered the fray, and they were blunt in attack. At least Ireland would get another chance to hone their skills against beatable opposition. For Ramsey and England, the tournament favourites and number one seeds awaited.

ENGLAND: *Gordon Banks; Jimmy Armfield, Jack Charlton, Bobby Moore, Ray Wilson (Stuart Pearce 78); Stanley Matthews, Duncan Edwards, Bobby Charlton, Tom Finney (Bryan Robson 54); Gary Lineker, Jimmy Greaves (Kevin Keegan 76)*
Subs not used: *Peter Shilton, David Beckham*
Goal: *B Charlton 51*

REP. OF IRELAND: *Pat Bonner; John Carey, Paul McGrath, Mark Lawrenson, Denis Irwin; Johnny Giles, Roy Keane, Liam Brady (Ronnie Whelan 75), Steve Heighway; John Aldridge, Frank Stapleton (Niall Quinn 80)*
Subs not used: *Shay Given, David O'Leary, Ray Houghton*
Goal: *Aldridge 10*

71

THE ALL-TIME WORLD CUP

BRAZIL 4 SWEDEN 0

An emphatic start from the favourites. Four goals, two of them just divine, and a clean sheet to boot. The Swedes were never at the races.

It took a while for both sides to settle but once Brazil found their feet, the results were devastating. Starting with Didi (as most things did), through Rivelino, Pelé, Romario, back to Didi, and out to Garrincha, who skinned Erik Nilsson as he cut towards the goal. "Little Bird" waited to the last possible moment before unleashing Romario, who nonchalantly side-footed home.

Sweden were rocked back on their heels and Pelé's crew took advantage. Gren lost the ball in midfield, Rivelino fired a sharp pass into the box that Nordquist could only divert into Pelé's path. He made no mistake from 10 yards out. Hellström picked the ball out of the net. Two goals down, and that was the first time he'd touched the ball.

Towards the end of the half Sweden began to regain their composure. Nordahl imposed himself on Edinho, leading to an excellent chance for Skoglund who scuffed his shot wide. Hamrin ran at Nílton Santos with abandon; the great left-back was under pressure, if never completely out of control. Gren escaped Cerézo for long enough to loft a ball over Júlio César, but Gilmar was onto it before the disappointing Brolin.

Just before the break Brazil struck again, like some imperial power squashing an uprising. Garrincha cut through the middle and was upended by Liedholm. The Brazilians took what seemed like an age to decide who should take the free kick. Rivelino finally put the ball down and lashed it in from 25 yards. End of debate.

With the game effectively decided Zagallo brought on some reserves in the second half. Gérson for Didi, Ademir for Romario, and Zagallo himself for Rivelino. The battle for places was well and truly on. The supporting cast took their cue. Zagallo helped Nílton Santos tame Hamrin; Gérson - who never seemed to be hurried - immediately dictated play. Ademir, one of the early greats who paved the way for Pelé, look irresistible. Romario was sharp, but it was hard to see how he'd regain his place. A quick turn past Nordquist preceeded a reverse pass to the overlapping Carlos Alberto, who released Pelé from the grips of Gustavsson. The great man stepped over the low cross and left Ademir to fire home. Hellström looked shell-shocked and sank to his knees as the crowd rose to its feet.

Brazil eased off after that but could easily have had two more - Zagallo and Gérson both went close. Nordahl continued the fight and at least exposed a potential Brazilian weakness. The centre of defence was vulnerable, but the Swedes were never likely to take advantage.

The stage had been set. It seemed that there'd be no false dawns from this Brazil side, which was every bit as exciting as the neutral fan had hoped. England were next up, and after the Ireland result, Zagallo would hardly be quaking in his freshly muddied boots. For Sweden, only a win would do against Ireland - a tough task but anything would be easier than this.

WORLD CUP FINAL 1958, STOCKHOLM

BRAZIL 5 SWEDEN 2

Strange as it seems today, Brazil were not overwhelming favourites to lift the World Cup in 1958. Brazil's form in the years leading up to the Cup wasn't too impressive. England had turned them over only a couple years previous for instance, and so although the Brazilians were a danger, the host country was viewed as an equally likely winner.

The ever-pragmatic Swedish authorities decided that players plying their trade abroad could represent the national team after all, having previously excluded several stars from the 1948 Olympic gold medal-winning side. The change of heart brought back several greats (Gren, Liedholm, Hamrin) and the Swedes duly progressed to the Final, only to find that they were suddenly big underdogs.

Brazil had looked solid defensively in their first group match against England but stepped up a gear once Coach Vicente Feola introduced two relative unknowns. Pelé and Garrincha entered the fray and Brazil were on their way. The Soviet Union were downed 2-0, plucky Wales fell 1-0 and a Pelé hat trick inspired Brazil to run over France 5-2 in a thrilling shoot-out with Fontaine and Kopa.

In the Final, Sweden made a dream start, Liedholm finishing a slick move between Bergmark, Börjesson and Simonsson. George Raynor probably hoped that his team of veterans would simply button down the hatches, but the Brazilian storm was too strong. The lead lasted just five minutes - the powerful Vavá scoring from close range. From then on, it was all Brazil. Vavá, preferred at centre-forward to Mazzola (who later starred in Italy under the name José Altafini), made it 2-1 after 32 minutes once Garrincha had again skinned his man.

All over the pitch Brazillian stars were shining brightly. Garrincha continued to torture poor Axbom, and Didi directed affairs from midfield.

The third goal was a classic. Pelé, just 17, controlled a Nílton Santos pass with his chest, chipped it over Gustavsson and flew around the giant Swede to volley past Svensson. The Times report got it just right: "Who can live with this sort of stuff?" Certainly not the Swedes.

Sweden's old warriors battled well, Gren in particular looked glad to be back on the international scene at 37, but the normal penetration from the wings was missing. Hamrin and Skoglund had been key figures in Sweden's earlier games, scoring five between them, but they were now up against possibly the finest full-back pairing ever. Feola introduced Djalma Santos specifically to deal with Skoglund, and that's precisely what he did. Namesake Nílton followed suit against Hamrin and the game was won.

There was time for a couple more gems, however. The energy of Mário Zagallo helped transform Brazil's 4-2-4 into a 4-3-3 when needed, and it was he who connected with a rebound to make it four before Simmonsson got one back.

Didi was the key figure, and player of the tournament, but it was clear that Pelé would soon be in a class all by himself. Sure enough, he had the final word. A header from Zagallo's cross made it 5-2 and Brazil, with perhaps the greatest team of all-time, became the first (and so-far only) team to win the World Cup on a foreign continent.

Didi

Today we most strongly associate Brazil's World Cup triumph of 1958 with the rise of Pelé, but at the time Didi was universally recognised as Brazil's - and possibly the world's - best player.

Didi played in three World Cup finals tournaments. In 1954, Didi had scored two goals in the group matches before becoming embroiled - along with everyone else - in the infamous "Battle of Berne" quarter-final with the great Hungarians. Four years later, the finals were treated to the finer side of Brazilian football, with Didi at the hub of things. Brazil had built upon Hungary's tactical revolution (using a deep lying centre-forward to create a 3-3-4 formation) and adapted it to a 4-2-4. Brazilian coach Vicente Feola employed one midfielder to win the ball (usually Zito) and one to use it. That was Didi's job, and few have ever done it more effectively. By 1958, he was nearly 30, having made his international debut in 1952, but in Sweden he was all but unstoppable. Brazil scored 11 goals en route to the final, and Didi had a significant hand in over half of them. Against Sweden in the deciding match, he ran the show, finding time and space like no one else could.

Also in 1958, Didi was transferred to Real Madrid, already legendary European Champions. An inside forward trio of Didi, Di Stefano and Puskas looked irresistible, but it didn't work. Legend has it that Di Stefano didn't take kindly to sharing top billing, but in reality it seems that there just wasn't enough space for two play-makers, both of whom liked to feed on-rushing team mates. Puskas also said that Didi's lack of pace didn't suit Madrid's style.

For Brazil, however, Didi didn't need speed of foot to make his mark. At the age of 33, he was again an important piece as Brazil retained the World Cup in 1962, even in the absence of the injured Pelé.

In all Didi scored 20 goals in 68 full internationals for Brazil. Many of his goals came by the way of the curled free kick or banana shot, which he pioneered.

Didi: Innovator, genius and winner.

THE ALL-TIME WORLD CUP

BRAZIL: *Gilmar; Carlos Alberto, Júlio César, Edinho, Nílton Santos; Garrincha, Cerezo, Didi (Gérson 45), Roberto Rivelino (Mário Zagallo 45); Pelé, Romario (Ademir 45)*
Subs not used: *Claudio Taffarel, Djalma Santos*
Goals: Romario 16, Pelé 19, Rivelino 44, Ademir 61

SWEDEN: *Ronnie Hellström; Orvar Bergmark, Bjorn Nordquist, Bengt Gustavsson, Erik Nilsson; Kurt Hamrin, Nils Liedholm, Gunnar Gren (Bo Larsson 70), Lennart Skoglund; Gunnar Nordahl, Tomas Brolin (Sven Rydell 69)*
Subs not used: *Thomas Ravelli, Patrik Andersson, Karl-Erik Palmér*

BRAZIL 1 ENGLAND 1

This was the tournament's first superpower summit, even if England hadn't looked like one so far.

This time they stepped up a few gears. It was enough, but just barely. Robson was retained with Charlton this time given the role of supporting Lineker. Greaves sat in the stands, perhaps ruing a miss or two against Ireland.

Brazil were unchanged, which was surprising given Ademir's debut. The central defensive pairing also remained in tact, but perhaps there weren't many viable alternatives.

It was England who took the early initiative, Edwards and Robson, quickly establishing themselves as twin terrors, lashing into Didi and Cerézo - supposedly the ball-winner but just overpowered here. Edwards charged forward and found Finney on the left. The Preston winger looped over a cross that Robson met with a diving header that Gilmar did well to touch on to the post. Nílton Santos cleared the rebound and immediately Brazil were on the attack. Didi, relishing the space that Robson had vacated, stroked a neat pass to Garrincha, who renewed his torment of Wilson and fired a cross-shot that Romario latched onto giving Banks no chance. From looking dangerous at one end, England had conceded at the other.

Bobby Moore, captain of a side already full of leaders, rallied his troops while keeping a firm check on Pelé. Matthews attacked down the right and forced a corner. Sir Stan swung it in himself, and Jack Charlton rose above Júlio César to equalise. Not particularly pretty, but well deserved.

Brazil immediately brought on Dunga for Cerézo in an effort to gain control of midfield. England retained the upper hand, but at least now they were in a fight. Brazil ended the first half on an upbeat note, Pelé finally turning Moore

Bobby Charlton

With a few strands of hair brushed across his balding head, Bobby Charlton was one of the world's most recognisable footballers, but it was his shooting rather than his hairstyle that grabbed most attention.

A record 49 goals in 106 internationals testifies to Charlton's goal scoring feats, but not to the great manner in which he scored them. When Bobby Charlton had the ball at his feet and the goal in his sights, the crowd were on the edge of their seats, hoping for, even expecting, a thunderbolt from one of the greatest long-range bombers ever.

For club and country, Charlton inspired great things, bringing both back from the low point of the late 1950s. Charlton survived the Munich air crash which claimed the lives of seven Manchester United players and thus deprived United - and England - the services of some exceptional players (Roger Byrne, Tommy Taylor, David Pegg, Eddie Coleman and of course Duncan Edwards). The loss slowed United's progress towards European glory and left England ill-equipped to compete in the 1958 World Cup, where Charlton was ill-advisedly left on the sidelines.

The England selectors made no such mistake four years later and Charlton starred as England progressed to the quarter-finals. Extremely versatile, Charlton played in every position across the England forward line bar outside right, and after shining in Chile on the left-wing, he soon moved inside.

Charlton didn't always dominate as a playmaker, but the threat of his goals demanded the utmost respect. When England faced West Germany in the 1966 World Cup Final, the Germans feared Charlton so much that Franz Beckenbauer was summoned to man-mark him. It was a close contest between two greats (although Beckenbauer was just beginning his odyssey), but Charlton was happy enough as England triumphed 4-2. European and English Footballer of the Year awards were fully justified.

With United, Charlton won the FA Cup in 1963 and three league titles, the last of which - in 1967 - served as a passport into the European Cup. Untied marched to the Final at Wembley where they dismantled Eusebio and Benfica 4-1, aided by two Charlton goals.

Charlton's departure from international football came in controversial circumstances. In the World Cup quarter-final against West Germany in 1970, England were cruising 2-0. Old rival Beckenbauer struck back in the 67th minute, after which Alf Ramsey almost immediately substituted

Charlton. West Germany went on to win 3-2 in extra time.

With a World Cup, a European Cup, and a European Championship third place finish, Charlton is the most successful, as well as the most famous of all English footballers. Only supporters of Bobby Moore and Stanley Matthews argue that he wasn't also the best.

only for his other nemesis, Banks, to parry from close range.

Ademir came on at half-time, as did Zagallo, and Brazil again looked fortified. Ramsey sent out the same side, but the momentum was gone. Ademir spun past Jack Charlton, foiled only by the covering Armfield. Garrincha jinked past poor Wilson but shot high and wide. At the other end, chances were few and far between. Charlton hit a bobbled shot from the edge of the area and Lineker nearly reached a Matthews cross, but there was only one likely winner now. Ramsey threw on Tommy Lawton near the end, hoping his aerial power would unsettle Brazil, but he never got a chance. Brazil's full-backs looked the best in the competition and if Matthews and Finney were never completely broken, they were certainly bent out of shape. David Beckham was introduced in the final minutes and looked comfortable enough to suggest that this wouldn't be the last we heard from him.

When the final whistle sounded, Moore looked disappointed, which was the measure of the man, but most England supporters were relieved. A loss would have left England in serious peril, and to concede just one goal against this Brazilian team was no mean feat. For Brazil, a reality check. Sure they looked the better team, possibly the best team of all, but they received warning that not everyone would lay down and die. If England had been resilient, what would the Germans or Italians do?

Both teams still had some work to do to ensure they progressed to the next round. Brazil's task seemed little more than a formality, but England would need to beat Sweden for the first time in over 30 years.

BRAZIL: *Gilmar; Carlos Alberto, Edinho, Júlio César, Nílton Santos; Garrincha, Cerézo (Dunga 38), Didi, Roberto Rivelino (Zagallo 45); Pelé, Romario (Ademir 45)*
Subs not used: *Claudio Taffarel, Djalma Santos*
Goal: *Romario 22*

ENGLAND: *Gordon Banks; Jimmy Armfield, Jack Charlton, Bobby Moore, Ray Wilson; Stanley Matthews, Bryan Robson, Duncan Edwards, Tom Finney (David Beckham 84); Bobby Charlton (Tommy Lawton 76); Gary Lineker*
Subs not used: *Peter Shilton, Billy Wright, Paul Gascoigne*
Goal: *Jack Charlton 35*

WORLD CUP QUARTER-FINAL, CHILE 1962

BRAZIL 3 ENGLAND 1

Brazil were World Champions, but were without Pelé and seemingly in decline. England had enjoyed one of their finest ever seasons in 1960-61 having successfully rebuilt after Munich. It looked like a chance for England to finally assert themselves on the world stage, but in actuality simply served as an indicator of what needed to be done if England were to challenge on home soil in 1966.

Brazil had looked good in their first game, a 3-0 whitewash over Mexico, but disaster struck in the 0-0 draw with a strong Czech team. Pelé's groin had given way, and Brazil were to be without their best player for the remainder of the tournament. It didn't seem to matter against Spain, however. Pelé's replacement Amarildo scored both goals in a 2-1 win and was beginning to look like a more than adequate stand-in for the injured superstar.

England's passage was altogether less comfortable. Outplayed by Hungary in the first game, they out-muscled Argentina in the second before holding Bulgaria to a 0-0 draw. England had done enough, but would need to step it up against Brazil.

They certainly had the players to make an impact. Jimmy Greaves and Booby Charlton were in their pomp up front, and a young Bobby Moore had recently been introduced at wing-half.

England also had a fine full-back pairing in Armfield and Wilson, but the latter was to meet any winger's nightmare in this match. Garrincha was in the mood. In the absence of Pelé, the outrageously gifted winger put Brazil on his back and opened the scoring with a header from a corner. England equalised through Gerry Hitchens but were soon undone by Garrincha's magic. He hit a thumping free kick that Springett blocked only for Vava, Brazil's powerful centre-forward, to put home the rebound.

Garrincha scored the third goal himself, with a swinging shot from outside the area that found the top corner.

Brazil, of course, went on to retain the title before the team fell into temporary decline. England, on the other hand were about to embark on their most fruitful era. The likes of Moore and Wilson would get better and new stars like Banks and Hurst would emerge. It was the end, however, for Johnny Haynes. The England inside-left, who'd formed the creative half of England's midfield pairing, was sacrificed. It was true that he'd failed to deliver at World Cup level, but he was unfairly burdened.

In 1961, when England thrashed Scotland 9-3, he'd been partnered with the stylish Booby Robson, who'd been able to share the creative load. But in Chile, with Moore and Ron Flowers at half-back, the responsibility lay entirely with Haynes and it was too much for him to carry. As the Yugoslavian manager said: "Number 10 takes the corners. Number 10 takes the throw-ins. So what do we do? We put a man on number 10. Goodbye England."

SWEDEN 3 REP. OF IRELAND 2

Both teams needed a win, which led to an exciting, all-action game. Ireland played above themselves again, but Sweden were better than they'd shown against Brazil.

Gren and Liedholm, who were out-gunned in their first match, finally found their feet and soon made an impact. Gren put Liedholm through, his pull-back blasted in by Nordahl, who deserved a goal for his efforts against Brazil.

After half an hour it was 2-0. Nordahl rose above Lawrenson and nodded past Bonner, who looked increasingly helpless.

Sweden might have gone on and killed the game, but Ireland's key players wouldn't go that easily. McGrath, who shone in two World Cups despite worn-out knees, dispossessed Brolin and played it out to Keane. A quick shimmy and Brady was clear. The play-maker nutmegged Nordqvist and chipped delicately over the advancing Hellström for a picture-book goal.

Ireland brought on Niall Quinn at half-time, hopeful that he'd have more luck against Gustavsson than Frank Stapleton. It was the other striker, Aldridge, who brought Ireland level, however. Johnny Giles, who'd been quiet until now, drove forward and released Heighway. He crossed before Bergmark could get there and Aldridge stabbed home the low ball at the near post.

The Irish were now full of confidence and looked for the winner. Keane came close with a long drive, and Carey nodded over from a corner - but Sweden weren't ones to be brushed aside.

Sweden lacked many things - particularly a World Class ball-winner - but they had some quality players and great belief. Encouraged by the twin pillars of Gustavsson at one end and Nordahl at the other, they forged on and eventually found a winner that kept them in the competition. Agne Simonsson was introduced and his 1958 connection with Kurt Hamrin was soon renewed. The little right-winger waltzed past Irwin and whipped in a cross. Nordahl got between McGrath and Lawrenson in the air to knock it down and Simonsson did the rest.

After coming back so bravely, Ireland had been denied at the last. After two games each, Group One was still anyone's to win. Sweden would be through if they beat England, although a draw would do as long as Brazil remained unbeaten. Ireland's task looked impossible. The maths were complicated, but they could simplify matters if they thrashed Brazil by three. You'd have to have been off your head to think it could happen, and even the Irish don't drink that much.

REP. OF IRELAND: *Pat Bonner; John Carey, Paul McGrath, Mark Lawrenson, Denis Irwin; Johnny Giles, Roy Keane, Liam Brady (Billy Whelan 72), Steve Heighway; John Aldridge, Frank Stapleton (Niall Quinn 45)*
Subs not used: *Shay Given, David O'Leary, Ray Houghton*
Goals: *Brady 36, Aldridge 62*

SWEDEN: *Ronnie Hellström; Orvar Bergmark, Bjorn Nordquist, Bengt Gustavsson, Erik Nilsson; Kurt Hamrin, Gunnar Gren, Nils Liedenhom, Lennart Skoglund (Bo Larsson 77); Tomas Brolin (Agne Simonsson 72), Gunnar Nordahl*
Subs not used: *Thomas Ravelli, Patrik Andersson, Jonas Thern, Sven Rydell*
Goals: *Nordahl 22, 29, Simonsson 76*

ENGLAND 3 SWEDEN 1

Buoyed by the draw with Brazil, England set out to impose themselves on weaker opponents. Ramsey was still tinkering with the line-up. This time he switched to a 4-3-3 with David Beckham joining the midfield and Bobby Charlton playing to the left of Lineker and Matthews.

Beckham immediately showed his worth, bursting past the promoted Larsson before a combination of Gren and Gustavsson bundled him over just outside the area. It looked like Charlton range but not even he hit free kicks like Beckham. Hellström could only deflect a crisp curling shot into the path of Lineker, who didn't miss from there.

Robson and Edwards again took over the crowded midfield (both sides with three in the middle and two out wide), and Charlton enjoyed life against Bergmark. A swerving run on the left ended with delicate cross, which Robson met with an athletic volley - Manchester United legends living it large on the greatest stage of all.

England pushed on, but Sweden had too many accomplished players to buckle entirely. Gunnar Nordahl, in particular, continued to cause problems.

Ramsey had chosen this match to see if Billy Wright could once again be the answer to England's problem at centre-back, which was a good idea, but bad timing. Nordahl dominated the shorter Wright in the air and was unlucky not to put his side back in the game just before half-time when Banks tipped over his sharp header.

After the break, England quickly put the result beyond doubt. Greaves - given a run in place of Wright in a re-shuffled line-up - took a pass from Beckham, shimmied past Nordquist and shot firmly underneath Hellström. Invisible one minute, cheeky and brilliant the next, which just about summed it up with Greavesie.

With Edwards now in defence Gren and Leidholm finally found some space in midfield. A pretty one-two saw Gren release Hamrin on the right. Nordahl met the low cross for his third goal of the tournament.

If Sweden were to stage a comeback, Hamrin would have to supply the ammunition. Arguably the key figure in 1958, and effective against Ireland, he had less success here. Garrincha might have had Wilson's number, but the England left-back was a fine defender - one of the best in the 1960s - and Hamrin couldn't break free.

Near the end, Matthews gave a lesson in how to beat a left-back. From a walking start he suddenly burst past Erik Nilsson and this time cut inside and shot firmly with his left. Hellström saved it well and didn't deserve to be humiliated, but a Matthews goal wouldn't have hurt.

Sweden and George Raynor were out having shown that organisation and a plethora of quality players only goes so far when faced with an assortment of greats. England were through after a shaky start and looked increasingly comfortable. The fun, however, had only just begun. Next up, a quarter-final against Germany.

ENGLAND: *Gordon Banks; Jimmy Armfield, Billy Wright (Jimmy Greaves 50), Bobby Moore (Tony Adams 83), Ray Wilson; David Beckham, Bryan Robson, Duncan Edwards; Stanley Matthews, Gary Lineker, Bobby Charlton*
Subs not used: *Peter Shilton, Tom Finney, Paul Gascoigne*
Goals: *Lineker 12, Robson 26, Greaves 56*

SWEDEN: *Ronnie Hellström; Orvar Bergmark, Bjorn Nordquist (Knut Nordahl 72), Bengt Gustavsson, Erik Nilsson; Kurt Hamrin, Bo Larsson (Agne Simonsson 66), Gunnar Gren, Nils Liedholm, Lennart Skoglund; Gunnar Nordahl*
Subs not used: *Thomas Ravelli, Sven Rydell, Roland Neilsson*
Goal: *G Nordahl 71*

BRAZIL 5 REP. OF IRELAND 1

Brazil - who were already through barring a disaster - rested several players and unleashed a second tier of world-beaters.

Ireland had looked a dangerous side in their first two games, but they were ill-equipped to deal with Brazil, even the reserves. Garrincha gave way to Jairzinho, who continued Irwin's nightmare. Ademir finally got a start and looked to torture test the fancied McGrath and Lawrenson. Pelé was also rested, with Rondaldo taking his place, while Gérson would make the play in the absence of Didi.

Ireland's options weren't so lavish. If Brazil's changes hinted that Zagallo thought they were already through, Charlton's move seemed to confirm that he agreed with the assessment. The attack-minded Heighway was replaced on the left by the defensive Ronnie Whelan - a move designed to stifle Jairzinho rather than threaten Carlos Alberto.

The plan never looked like working from the moment Jairzinho charged past both Whelan and Irwin and thrashed a high shot past the unfortunate Bonner.

Ademir was up next, exchanging passes with Ronaldo, before he weaved past Lawrenson and chipped the keeper.

On the half hour mark, Zagallo - starting for Rivelino - pushed Carey back and knocked a pass inside for Gérson. The balding, smoking, left-footed genius floated a cross to the far right. Jairzinho latched on and locked in. Bonner was equal to his headed attempt this time, but Ronaldo poked in the rebound.

Ireland's feisty midfielders looked bewildered. Rarely can Keane and Giles have been so effectively sidelined. Giles - not looking too comfortable on the right - was blotted out by Nílton Santos - while Keane was working overtime to try and cool Gérson's fire.

To add to the problems, Ireland's front pair looked more impotent than ever. Djalma Santos was played in the centre of defence in the hope of solving Brazil's one problem. It certainly seemed to work here as he completely overwhelmed Stapleton. Aldridge of course remained a danger in the box, but he wasn't likely to create an opening for himself. Alan Hansen described him as "one of the worst five-a-side players I ever came across", which sounded harsh but was probably fair enough.

After 40 minutes, a ray of hope for Ireland. Keane shrugged off Dunga and hit a rasping effort past Gilmar, who might have done better. There was no question that by comparison with some other Brazilian keepers, Gilmar looked pretty special, but a Yashin or Banks he was not.

After the break, Zagallo made more changes. The famous Zico replaced

Gérson, while Zito came on for Dunga. The new midfield partnership didn't start too well. Zico's errant pass was snapped up by Giles, Brady flew by the lead-footed Zito, only for substitute Billy Whelan - a Busby Babe - to miscue his shot.

Zico immediately made amends, running at the heart of the Ireland defence and laying it off to Ademir, who finished coolly.

Brazil's fifth was altogether less pretty. Substitute Roberto Carlos stabbed home after Djalma Santos had caused havoc from a Zagallo corner.

Ireland were praying for mercy by the end, and Ronaldo obliged, missing from a Jairzinho cross. The buoys from the Emerald Isle were thoroughly outclassed, but continue to battle to the end. Ireland were out but were not totally disgraced. Keane, McGrath and Brady looked like they belonged, at least in patches.

Brazil were through in style. Five goals scored with nonchalant ease, and with Pelé and Garrincha sat in the stands. Terrifying.

BRAZIL: *Gilmar; Carlos Alberto, Djalma Santos, Júlio César, Nílton Santos (Roberto Carlos 72); Jairzinho, Dunga (Zito 45), Gérson (Zico 45), Mário Zagallo; Ronaldo, Ademir*
Sub not used: *Claudio Taffarel, Rivaldo*
Goals: *Jairzinho 11, Ademir 14, 51, Ronaldo 30, Roberto Carlos 79*

REP. OF IRELAND: *Pat Bonner; John Carey, Paul McGrath, Mark Lawrenson, Denis Irwin; Johnny Giles, Roy Keane, Liam Brady, Ronnie Whelan (Billy Whelan 68); John Aldridge, Frank Stapleton (Robbie Keane 85)*
Subs not used: *Shay Given, David O'Leary, Steve Heighway*
Goals: *Roy Keane 40*

GROUP ONE DETAILS AND RESULTS

	P	W	D	L	F	A	GD	Pts
BRAZIL	3	2	1	0	10	2	8	7
ENGLAND	3	1	2	0	5	3	2	5
SWEDEN	3	1	0	2	4	9	-5	3
IRELAND	3	0	1	2	4	9	-5	1

Brazil and England qualify for quarter-finals

THE MATCHES

Results

England	1-1	Rep. of Ireland
Brazil	4-0	Sweden
England	1-1	Brazil
Rep. of Ireland	2-3	Sweden
Sweden	1-3	England
Brazil	5-1	Rep. of Ireland

Goal scorers

Three goals: Gunnar Nordahl (Sweden), Ademir (Brazil)

Two goals: John Aldridge (Ireland), Romario (Brazil), Bobby Charlton (England),

One goal each: Pelé, Roberto Rivelino, Jairzinho, Ronaldo, Roberto Carlos (all Brazil), Jimmy Greaves, Gary Lineker, Bryan Robson (all England), Roy Keane, Liam Brady (both Rep. of Ireland), Agne Simonssen (Sweden)

GROUP TWO:
Austria, France, Germany, Spain

The second group brought together four western European sides, each with a strong football heritage. France, three-time semi-finalists and one-time winner, can also lay claim to a major role in establishing the World Cup in the first place. It wasn't called the Jules Rimet trophy for nothing (Rimet was FIFA president from 1920 to 1954).

Austria also had successful sides, in 1934 and again twenty years later. Since then, the Austrians have qualified well but made little impact on the finals themselves.

Spain's major contributions to football's history have been made away from the World Cup. Real Madrid helped galvanise the European Cup's reputation by winning it the first five times, and the Spanish were among the first to take the European Championship seriously too. At the big dance, however, not a lot of joy, although Spain always seem to be a fancied team.

Germany are also perennial favourites, but with good reason. West Germany participated in every tournament between 1954 and 1990. Three wins, three losses in the Final and one other semi-final appearance paints a picture of consistent dominance - which is absolutely right. Strangely, the united Germany has faired less well. Two quarter-final losses in 1994 and 1998 followed a first round loss in 1938 and a semi-final appearance in 1934. Still, 1938 is the only time the Germans have ever failed to get through at least one round, and the only time they finished with a losing record in the finals. Even the East Germans managed to progress to the second phase in 1974, trumping their Western neighbours along the way.

As you'd expect with such a perennial contender, the Germans have met each of their Group Two opponents at least once in the World Cup finals.

Nearby Austria have been a favourite opponent. Four meetings, yielding three German victories (1934, 1954 and 1982) and one Austrian upset (1978). Worryingly for Austria, the first two defeats came over their vintage teams. The 1982 meeting is forever clouded in allegations of conspiracy. The 1-0 result for West Germany guaranteed both advanced at the expense of the outraged Algerians.

France have faced Germany (West) three times, thrashing them 6-3 in the third-place play-off in 1958 and losing two semi-finals in 1982 and 1986, the first on penalties. Several players involved in those tight games would face off again; Matthäus, Brehme, Rummenigge and Förster for Germany; Bats, Bossis, Tigana and Platini for France. Kopa, Fontaine, Walter and Rahn had rendezvoused in 58.

France have faced Austria twice, losing in 1934 and winning in 1982. Krankl, Koncilia and Pezzey would meet familiar opposition.

Strange as it might seem, France have never met Spain in the World Cup finals. The Spanish track record against its other Group 2 rivals is less than promising. A 2-1 loss to Krankl and friends in 1978, and defeats by the same score at the hands of West Germany in 1966 and 1982, before regaining a little pride via a draw with Germany in 1994.

The Germans were obviously the group's form horse and had a squad capable of hammering home its advantage. France would also be dangerous - on a role after 1998. Spain and Austria would look to beat each other and upset the apple cart against the big boys. The likes of Gento and Suárez and Ocwirk and Sindelar at least gave them a puncher's chance.

FRANCE 3 SPAIN 0

There were those who wondered how this French team might gel, but they were given a definitive answer here. Both sides relied heavily on players from the last twenty years and that was bad news for Spain.

Platini, Kopa and particularly Zidane picked their way through the Spanish defence, and it took a classic performance from Zamora to keep things decent.

From the outset, the French looked the sharper, a more cohesive unit. Kopa ferreted down the right, cut inside Camacho, before shooting just firmly and forcing Zamora to tip it around the left hand post. The reprieve was temporary. Zidane released an overlapping Bossis, who cut it back for Platini to let fly from the edge of the area. Zamora didn't move.

Spain awoke for long enough to allow Gento to show his wares, nipping past Thuram and supplying a cross for Zarra, who reacted slowly. The imperious Desailly intervened. Platini then turned provider. Jinking past Guardiola, he slid a smooth pass in front of Fontaine, who found Spain's central defenders to be slightly ponderous. Zamora was again left helpless.

Spain made adjustments at half-time. Pirri came on, adding ballast to midfield, and for a while the game lost its way. Zidane soon got things back on track, holding off Pirri before Hierro brought him down in the area. Fontaine took the tournament's first penalty and Spain were beaten. Gento was taken off 15 minutes from the end but it was hard to tell if the Spanish coach was disappointed in him, or simply protecting a great player from further humiliation.

Suárez showed a glimpse of what he could do with ten minutes to go - skinning Deschamps and forcing a crisp save from Bats. It looked pretty, but

Spain needed more for their main man. Michel was disappointing too, tamed by Bossis, who seemed to have sealed his place in the starting XI.

Tigana, who'd been relatively quiet, provided Fontaine with a final chance, but Zamora wasn't in the mood to be embarrassed and saved well. It looked like he'd be well employed during Spain's visit to the tournament.

There didn't appear to be many options for José Villalonga. He'd put out what looked like his best side and it had capitulated before his eyes. The likes of Amancio or Raul might have some answers, but there wasn't a World Cup giant ready to fill the breach.

France's opening shot had been emphatic. Thoroughly outplaying a team that was over-rated, but shouldn't have been this bad. Germany would have watched them carefully, but there weren't any visible dents in the berets just yet.

FRANCE: *Joel Bats; Lilian Thuram, Marcel Desailly, Robert Jonquet, Maxime Bossis; Jean Tigana, Didier Deschamps (Alain Giresse 88); Raymond Kopa (Jean-Pierre Papin 76), Michel Platini, Zinedine Zidane; Just Fontaine*
Subs not used: *Fabian Barthez, Manuel Amaros, Roger Piantoni*
Goals: *Platini 16, Fontaine 32, 60*

SPAIN: *Ricardo Zamora; Albert Ferrer, Fernando Hierro, Antonio Maceda (Sergi 68), José Camacho; Michel, Josep Guardiola, Luis Suárez, Francisco Gento (Rafael Gordillo 75); Emilio Butragueno (Pirri 45), Zarra*
Subs not used: *Andoni Zubizarreta, Amancio Amaro*

Raymond Kopa and Just Fontaine

The 1958 World Cup links the careers of these two great French forwards. Fontaine scored 13 goals in Sweden, a record that is unlikely to be broken, but it says a great deal that it was Kopa who was crowned European Footballer of the Year.

Kopa acted as Fontaine's own personal supply line, providing the through balls that Fontaine relished.

In the group stages, Moroccan-born Fontaine scored a hat-trick against Paraguay, two in defeat by Yugoslavia and another while downing Scotland 2-1. Kopa scored two himself, one set up by Fontaine. There were another two Fontaine goals in the quarter-final and even one when losing to Brazil, before rounding things off with four (and one for Kopa) in the third-place Play-off.

Fontaine hadn't even been expected to play in the World Cup - he was a reserve and came in only when René Biliard was injured. Sadly, his own career was ravaged by injury too. He was forced to retire in 1961 after a second broken leg. Until then, however, he was all but unstoppable.

He continued his spree with France after the World Cup and for Reims, who he propelled to the European Cup Final in 1959. By the end, he'd scored 30 goals in 21 Internationals.

If Fontaine was something of an overnight sensation, Kopa was an established star by the time of the World Cup, having made his debut with France in 1952. He went on to win 45 caps and score 17 goals.

Kopa also starred with Reims and led them to the first European Cup Final in 1956. Shortly afterwards Kopa joined Real Madrid, who had won the inaugural competition. He featured alongside Di Stefano and Gento as his new team collected the next three European Cups. Despite the success many felt that Kopa's talents were somewhat wasted in Madrid; Real had Di Stefano at centre-forward and (from summer 1958) Puskas as inside left, so the versatile Kopa was played on the right wing.

He resumed an inside- or centre-forward role when he returned to Reims in 1959 and was reunited with Fontaine.

Together, Fontaine and Kopa formed one of the most lethal striking partnerships ever. In Platini and Zidane, France have found successors to Kopa and his magical ball skills but, as yet, are still searching for a goal scoring machine to match Fontaine.

GERMANY 1 AUSTRIA 1

A surprising start from one of the World Cup's giants. Strangely tame, Germany simply couldn't find a way to break down a stubborn Austrian unit. Schön was confident his side had all the ingredients; he'd also consulted his senior players as he was rumoured to have done in 1974. Their advice wasn't so magical this time.

The first half was a dull affair, with neither side able to gain control of midfield. If Germany thought Matthäus and his cohorts were going to overpower opponents in this competition, the impressive Ocwirk and Sindelar persuaded otherwise. Combining a tall, strong and smooth centre-half with a slender, crafty centre-forward looked like a masterstroke from Meisl, who put one over on his opposite number.

It was Austria who made the first chance. Alfred Körner whizzed down the left and Ocwirk arrived late to test Maier. Ocwirk was involved again shortly afterwards. Strolling past Walter in midfield, he released Hasil whose aim was way off. Twenty-five minutes in and Germany hadn't had a shot. Suddenly, as if bored by the proceedings, Helmut Rahn intervened. Picking up the ball on the left, he charged across the area and blasted a rising shot past Koncilia. No one was too surprised, but the Germans knew they'd gotten out of jail.

Austria continued to push forward. Sindelar created a chance for Binder, and Happel appeared from the back to head over a corner. Meisl had used Krankl to mark Beckenbauer every time the sweeper got the ball, and Germany's ability to forge attack from defence was severely stifled.

The half-time break brought a change to the game's pattern. Schön moved Beckenbauer into midfield where he immediately stamped his authority. Sammer looked smooth as a replacement at the back and the German machine was firing again. Rahn tortured Sara on the left, pulling back a neat ball for Müller, who missed his first chance of the tournament. Rummenigge finally got involved, exchanging passes with Beckenbauer before testing Koncilia once more. The tide had well and truly turned and Germany looked set to burst the damn.

Ocwirk was still there though, keeping tabs on Matthäus, and again started an attack. Binder shot straight at Maier, who did well to stop it but couldn't hang on. The prolific Josef Bican, on as a substitute, did the rest.

It was all Germany after that, but Austria held on. Matthäus stormed forward, skipped past Pezzey before the impressive Hanappi stepped in. Müller rose well to meet a Brehme cross but glanced it just wide. Moments later, he scooped another shot over the bar and it was clearly not going to be his day.

Rahn made one final effort, but was running out of steam. A strong run outside Sara was ruined by a tame cross-cum-shot.

Austria celebrated at the end, as well they should have. This was a true shock, and one that seriously endangered the second favourites. On this evidence, France might just turn them over in the next match, and if that happened, the unthinkable...

Austria had real hope. A win against Spain looked a distinct possibility and no neutral would complain if they got to see a little more of Ocwirk and Sindelar, true greats who looked every inch at home.

GERMANY: *Sepp Maier; Berti Vogts, Karlheinz Förster, Franz Beckenbauer, Andreas Brehme; Lothar Matthäus, Fritz Walter (Matthias Sammer 48), Wolfgang Overath; Karl-Heinz Rummenigge (Jürgen Klinsmann 77), Gerd Müller, Helmut Rahn.*
Subs not used: *Jürgen Croy, Jürgen Kohler, Günter Netzer*
Goal: *Rahn 28*

Austria: *Fritz Koncilia; Robert Sara, Bruno Pezzey, Ernst Happel, Gerhard Hanappi; Franz Hasil, Ernst Ocwirk, Matthias Sindelar, Alfred Körner; Franz Binder, Hans Krankl (Josef Bican 70)*
Subs not used: *Rudi Hiden, Erich Obermayer, Herbert Prohaska, Karl Koller*
Goal: *Bican 72*

Franz Beckenbauer

In the 1960s and 1970s as a player - and in the 1980s and 1990s as a coach - Franz Beckenbauer proved himself to be the ultimate winner, and is arguably the most successful figure in football history.

As a smooth midfielder or sweeper, for Bayern Munich and West Germany, Beckenbauer won all the game had to offer. Captain when West Germany lifted the World Cup in 1974, he had previously won runners-up and third-place medals in 1966 and 1970. At the European Championships, he lifted the trophy in 1972 and was a losing finalist four years later. At club level, Bayern won three consecutive European Champions Cups under the "Kaiser's" leadership, as well as a Cup-winners Cup, World Club Cup and a plethora of domestic honours.

But even after retiring as a player Beckenbauer continued to feed his incredible winning habit. In his first job as a coach, he guided an unexceptional West Germany side to the World Cup Final. Four years later, he repeated the trick and this time his team lifted the trophy, thus making Beckenbauer the only man to both captain and coach a World Cup winner.

For all his medals, however, Beckenbauer's great impact was his tactical innovation. In the 1960s and 1970s the game became faster and more aggressive, and time and space became precious commodities. Teams were forced to find new ways to break down obstinate defences. For Bayern, and eventually for West Germany, the answer was moving Beckenbauer into defence. From his sweeper position Beckenbauer could read the game and - when appropriate - launch attacks from the back where he was afforded more room to operate.

His legacy is such that today virtually every successful team uses a ball-playing defender, but Beckenbauer remains the original and the best.

Voted European Footballer of the Year in 1972 and 1976, Beckenbauer is one of only two defenders to win the award - an appropriate distinction for the greatest sweeper of all-time.

AUSTRIA 1 SPAIN 1

After two heart-racing opening fixtures, a more sedate encore. Spain finally came out to play, seemingly unimpressed by Austria's excellent start to the competition.

Spanish morale received an early boost. Gento, who'd at least looked a little ambitious against France, ran at Sara, attacking what Spain had clearly identified as Austria's soft underbelly. A neat cross followed and Zarra rose above Pezzey to give Spain their first goal of the competition. Hiden, introduced in favour of Koncilia, must have wished he'd stayed at home.

Austria had come from behind before however, and began to find their feet. Ocwirk was again excellent, duelling with Suárez and making the play. Austria's left-wing also sensed weakness and went past Chendo, forcing Hierro to come across and save the day. From the resulting corner Ocwirk got the first touch and Franz Binder fired home.

The game then settled into a pattern. One team would have a spell on top before submitting authority to the other. Spain looked more assured with Amancio Amaro helping out in midfield and Michel was more impressive this time. Suarez was still quiet but managed a tricky back heel from which Amancio should have done better.

Soon it was Austria's turn. Sindelar - to this point kept quiet by Guardiola - turned sharply just outside the area and fed Bican who had a screamer saved by Zamora. The new Austrian front pairing looked dangerous - two 1930s goal poachers, eagerly sniffing out opportunities.

Spain's cutting edge was not quite so sharp. Zarra continued to harass Pezzey, but lacked support. Raul came on just before half-time and should have helped, but taking off Amancio was a strange move.

The interval saw further changes on both sides. Meisl reshuffled his defence. Hanappi switched to the right to look after Gento with Karl Koller coming in on the left. Spain brought on Basora to add width on the right, with Michel moving inside.

As the second half progressed it was obvious that Meisl had gotten the better of Villalonga. Hanappi quietened Spain's main threat while Koller did just enough against the lively Basora. Michel didn't have much luck in the middle, outplayed by Ocwirk and Sindelar.

Franz Hasil finally got into the game after an hour, providing a penetrating cross from the right that Binder might have connected with but for Maceda's close attendance. Soon it was Spain's turn to threaten. Raul evaded Happel and fed Basora, who pulled his shot across the face of the goal. Zarra slid in but couldn't reach it.

92

Hanappi - looking even more assured on the right - soon tipped the scales again. He overlapped Hasil to tee up Sindelar who forced Zamora back into action. If there was compensation for Spain's poor showing it was that the great Zamora got plenty of exposure.

Austria looked the more likely to score near the end, but Spain's central defenders were more assured than against France.

A draw didn't really help either side, though it ensured Spain wouldn't be whitewashed. Austria could still qualify if they beat France, which seemed improbable even after watching Germany's first two games. The Austrian midfield, however, would relish its next test and already looked one of the best on show.

AUSTRIA: *Rudi Hiden; Robert Sara (Karl Koller 45), Bruno Pezzey, Ernst Happel, Gerhard Hanappi; Franz Hasil (Herbert Prohaska 78), Ernst Ocwirk, Matthias Sindelar, Alfred Körner; Franz Binder, Josef Bican*
Subs not used: *Fritz Koncilia, Erich Obermayer, Hans Krankl*
Goal: *Binder 28*

SPAIN: *Ricardo Zamora; Chendo (Albert Ferrer 80), Fernando Hierro, Antonio Maceda, José Camacho; Michel, Josep Guardiola, Amancio Amaro (Raul 40), Luis Suárez (Estanislao Basora 45), Francisco Gento; Zarra*
Subs not used: *Antonio Ramallets, Sergi*
Goal: *Zarra 16*

GERMANY 4 FRANCE 2

Germany needed a win and set about their business with the efficiency we've come to expect. France, who'd looked positively divine against Spain, were all at sea as soon as the Germans set on them.

It started well for France. Thuram moved down the right and fooled Maier with a floated pass to the back post that hit the crossbar. Fontaine was on hand for his third of the competition.

If disaster seemed imminent, no one had told Matthäus. After a quiet first match, he simply took command here. Heartened by Beckenbauer's assistance in midfield, he crushed Platini with a clean tackle on the half way line. Leaping to his feet, he evaded Deschamps and then set off towards the French goal. Bats braced himself for a pile-driver, so Matthäus slotted a ball through for Müller, who hesitated before side-footing home.

France now looked under pressure. If Müller was generally well contained by Desailly, then Bossis had no answer for an onrushing Rummenigge, and Schuster was too much for Deschamps. Introduced to manufacture some flair, the blonde German did just that.

The Germans were setting a tremendous pace, not really their style, but not at all to the liking of Kopa and Platini, whose quiet showing again raised questions about his World Cup pedigree.

Beckenbauer gave Germany the lead shortly before half-time. A neat combination with Rummenigge freed him from Blanc and the "Kaiser" made his mark. Bats might have done better, but Beckenbauer had imposed his will.

Jacquet - who didn't seem the type to panic - made only one change at half-time, moving Desailly into midfield to take care of Schuster and inserting Lizarazu at left-back.

The substitution had its desired impact. Schuster didn't enjoy his new companion and was soon removed. There were deadly side-effects, however. Bossis was now responsible for Müller, who seemed absolutely delighted. First he glanced in a Brehme cross and then from the restart he received Matthäus's pass, turned his man and completed his hat-trick. Jacquet had inadvertently taught every other team a lesson - if you find a way to stop a deadly marksman, don't leave the job half finished.

Desailly resumed responsibility after that, but the damage was done. Netzer, revelling in a tackle-free midfield, squeezed past Bossis and set up Rummenigge, who should have made it five.

The match was over and Schön eased off the gas. Matthäus and Beckenbauer were withdrawn and Zidane re-emerged, chipping a sweet shot onto the bar. Lizarazu scored from the partial clearance.

Overath, keen on regaining his place, came close at the end, and Sammer's long-range effort was well met by Bats.

Neither team looked much like it had in the first round of matches. It was hard to tell which was the more accurate picture, but the Germans seemed to have found their stride and it was hard to imagine them easing off now.

For the French, something to think about. How to make best use of their obvious talents? Platini, Zidane and Kopa had prospered against timid Spain, but faced with Matthäus and Beckenbauer, they'd gone eerily quiet.

Germany had now drawn with a gutsy - if over-matched - Austria and thrashed a skilled but overpowered France. Spain were next, and were almost irrelevant, but what would happen when Schön's team faced an opponent with enough weapons to do harm, and sufficient will to use them?

THE MATCHES

GERMANY: *Sepp Maier; Berti Vogts, Matthias Sammer, Karlheinz Förster, Andreas Brehme; Franz Beckenbauer (Wolfgang Overath 73), Lothar Matthäus (Willy Schulz 74), Bernd Schuster (Günter Netzer 71); Karl-Heinz Rummenigge, Gerd Müller, Helmut Rahn*
Subs not used: *Jürgen Croy, Jürgen Klinsmann*
Goals: *Müller 28, 60, 61, Beckenbauer 42*

FRANCE: *Joel Bats; Lilian Thuram, Marcel Desailly, Robert Jonquet, Maxime Bossis; Jean Tigana, Didier Deschamps (Alain Giresse 88); Raymond Kopa (Bixente Lizarazu 47), Michel Platini, Zinedine Zidane; Just Fontaine (Jean-Marie Papin 82)*
Subs not used: *Fabian Barthez, Roger Piantoni*
Goals: *Fontaine 16, Lizarazu 72*

WORLD CUP SEMI-FINAL 1982, SEVILLE

WEST GERMANY 3 FRANCE 3
(5-4 on penalties)

This was one of the most dramatic matches in World Cup history, with four extra time goals, a horrific challenge, and the competition's first ever penalty shoot-out.

West Germany were European Champions and highly fancied before the tournament began but had made quiet progress in this tournament. Following a defeat by Algeria, they'd recovered to knock four past Chile but subsequently returned to their dour ways.

The lacklustre display was in part due to the injury afflicting Karl-Heinz Rummenigge, the team's only truly great player. The blonde striker scored four goals in his first two games but started this match on the bench.

France had also looked unimpressive. It said something about this World Cup's double group stage system that a team could make the World Cup semi-finals having lost to England, drawn with Czechoslovakia and beaten only Kuwait, Northern Ireland and Austria. The team had plenty of stars, but in truth was probably a couple of years away from its peak. Their leader, the marvellous Michel Platini, would win the first of three European Footballer of the Year awards the next year.

The semi-final started briskly. Breitner released Fischer, whose shot was saved by Ettori, only for little Littbarski to slot home the opener. Within ten minutes it was level. Bernd Förster brought down Rocheteau and Platini

95

made no mistake from the spot.

The next hour passed without a goal, but not without incident. In one of the most famous atrocities in the World Cup, Patrick Battiston suffered a concussion that looked extremely serious after Harald Schumacher violently checked him with an aerial challenge as he ran through on goal. Fans and critics called it an assault and a disgrace; the referee didn't even give a foul.

Extra time came after Amoros hit the bar in the final minute, and then the fun really began. France struck first, Trésor volleying home after just three extra minutes. German coach Jupp Derwall decided it was time for a gamble and Rummenigge was introduced. Before he could get involved, however, France had scored another, the impressive Giresse firing one in off the post. Within four minutes Rummenigge had given his side hope with a tap in, and set up the equaliser with a cross for Fischer. All credit to Karl-Heinz; a true talisman performing under pressure. It looked like genius from Derwall but to be fair, the French coach had few options. Battiston's injury had exhausted the quota of substitutes.

The shoot-out was tense as always, perhaps more so because they were a World Cup novelty. Didier Six had a chance to finish it after Stielike missed. Bossis then failed for the French, to allow Hrubesch to seal it. Poor Bossis wouldn't be the last penalty fall-guy, and this wouldn't be the last time the Germans advanced in such dramatic circumstances.

Italy waited in the Final, however, and even German efficiency (and luck) couldn't deny a certain Paolo Rossi. But that was meagre compensation for the stylish French and the unfortunate Battiston.

FRANCE 2 AUSTRIA 1

A draw would do for France but they knew they were better than that. Platini decided this was the day to impose himself and even Ocwirk was unable to stop him. Combining beautifully with Zidane, the Juventus legend put on a show.

It started with a 30-yard pass to Kopa who knocked a first time volley into the box. Fontaine was there (as ever) but was beaten out by Happel. Next, Platini wrong-footed Ocwirk and Hasil before striking a sweet shot just over the bar.

With Platini setting the mood, the other French artists joined in. Zidane shared in a nifty one-two with his captain before displaying his immense strength to hold off Pezzey and chip home over the advancing Hiden.

Within ten minutes the lead was doubled, Kopa beat Koller on the right and

MARIO ZAGALLO

As coach of the team with the most abundant resources, Zagallo just had to keep the Brazilian juggernaut on track to lift the All-Time World Cup. That he managed to do so, however, was no mean feat. Accommodating the likes of Pelé, Ademir, Garrincha, Didi and Rivelino in one side took a minor miracle. Fortunately for Brazil, Zagallo knows all about miracles and even found time to make a few important cameos on the wing. A giant - on and off the pitch.

ROY KEANE

Keane's powerful displays in midfield kept Ireland in games, which by rights they should have lost by a distance. The draw against England was a major coup, especially for Keane, up against some of the greatest midfielders in the history of the game. Sweden and Brazil escaped with wins, but the likes of Gren and Gérson knew they'd been in a brawl.

KENNY DALGLISH

If only Jock Stein could have found a way to get Kenny to perform at his Liverpool best, perhaps the Scots would have stood a fighting chance. As it was Dalglish did better than in his previous World Cup appearances, and even looked pretty good on occasions. But the defences of Italy and Uruguay were of the highest order and provided a hostile environment in which to rebuild a World Cup reputation.

EUSEBIO AND FIGO

Portugal's main creator and finisher had some success during the All-Time World Cup, but were ultimately out-gunned by the stars of Argentina and Holland. Eusébio's speed and strength helped him continue his fine goal scoring record, even if he wasn't able to find a way to win games. A little more service from Figo might have helped, but the midfield battles were tough in this tournament, and in Krol, Marzolini and Onopko, the Portuguese midfielder received some top quality attention.

BOBBY CHARLTON

England's most important player, Charlton switched effortlessly
between midfield, up front and the wing. Wherever he played he
carried his country's greatest threat. His long-range strike against
Ireland marked the card of every defence in the competition. The
Germans were so impressed that their top terrier Bertie Vogts was
eventually dispatched to keep Charlton quiet. The ploy worked and
England were on their way out.

DAVID BECKHAM

He took a while to break into the line-up, but by the end of the All-Time World Cup, Beckham had demonstrated that he is completely at home playing with, and against, the game's greatest figures. His long-range passes and wondrous free-kicks translated well at All-Time level, and but for Sepp Maier, the old Beckham-to-Owen combination would have stolen the headlines again.

DANIEL PASSARELLA

If Argentina's brilliant team had a weakness it was in defence. Although the entire back line was world class, only Silvio Marzolini and the magnificent Passarella were true all-time greats. Silvio Piola finally found Argentina out in the air, but until then, Passarella's commanding displays kept things under control at the back while Maradona and Di Stefano did their thing up front.

DIEGO MARADONA

Occasionally over-shadowed by his teammate Di Stefano, Maradona
always seemed to be on hand when it counted most. If his team needed
a burst of genius, they knew where to turn. Several exhilarating runs,
numerous killer passes and a couple of spectacular goals lit up the
competition, even if Diego never quite dominated as in 1986.
Of course, his 87th minute goal gave Argentina another chance against
Italy, but even Maradona couldn't provide
the fairytale ending this time.

MICHEL PLATINI

As he did in the World Cups of 1978-1986, Platini drifted in and out of
the competition. When on song, however, the Frenchman made some
of the most compulsive viewing. Against Austria he ran the show,
eclipsing Ocwirk and Sindelar, and even his own superstar teammate
Zinedine Zidane. Platini had no answer against Holland, but he was
well looked after by the Dutch who clearly
identified him as the main threat.

MARCEL DESAILLY

Only one man effectively controlled Gerd Müller during the All-Time
World Cup. Desailly's combination of strength, pace and concentration
made him uniquely equipped to deal with the tournament's top scorer.
Unfortunately for France, Desailly was called away to other duties
during their match with Germany, and Müller took advantage. Other
top strikers were not so lucky. Marco van Basten and Zarra were
among those blotted out by the competition's number one stopper.

DINO ZOFF

Every keeper would have liked to play in front of the All-time Italian
defence, but few deserved it more than Dino Zoff. Known primarily for
his great longevity, Zoff's role in keeping out the greatest attacks in the
world shouldn't be underestimated. Important saves in virtually every
match were key to several close victories as Italy, and their greatest
custodian, progressed in typical style.

FRANCO BARESI

Commanding and controlling, Baresi was the leader of the All-Time
World Cup's meanest defence. In 1990 Franco swept behind Bergomi,
Ferri and Maldini and in front of Zenga. The All-Time team added Zoff
and Facchetti, and was virtually unbreakable. Baresi was at the centre
of it all again, presiding over affairs like the great general he was.

HOLLAND 1974

Van Hanegem, Neeskens, Krol, Suurbier and Cruyff - key players in 1974 and vital to Holland in the All-Time World Cup. If the Dutch underachieved in Munich, they did themselves justice here. The only team in the quarter-finals not containing a former World Cup winner (the Germans had 10), they progressed on talent alone until the old World Cup jinx struck again.

JOHANN CRUYFF

Sublime from start to finish, Cruyff's performances deserved to end
with a trophy, but it was just not meant to be for Johann in World
Cups. After leading his team all the way to the semis, Holland were
again upset by the Germans. Cruyff had a little more joy against Vogts
this time, but it made no odds. Beckenbauer and co. were not to be
denied and Cruyff was crushed again.

GERD MÜLLER

The All-Time World Cup's top scorer, Müller bagged eight in six
games - a pretty good strike rate but not anything special by his own
standards. As in his two World Cup finals appearances in 1970 and
1974, it was the timing of his scoring interventions that had most
impact. The at-the-death winner in the quarter-final broke English
hearts, and he was on the mark against Holland in the semis too.
Müller couldn't stop Brazil in the Final, despite scoring, but he 'd done
enough to underline his position as the ultimate World Cup goal scorer
and under-pressure-performer.

FRANZ BECKENBAUER

Switching between defence and midfield, Beckenbauer was one of the tournament's most influential figures. Until the Final, Germany kept finding ways to win, even against seemingly superior sides. The German captain was a crucial factor, plugging gaps wherever they appeared and driving his troops forward when the spectre of defeat loomed large. But then such performances are nothing new for the Kaiser, who in 30 years as a player and coach became a master in the art of winning.

PELE

The game's greatest player didn't disappoint when tested against the game's greats. When Brazil's fortunes were on the line, Pelé delivered. He produced the tournament's most dominant performance against Uruguay and scored twice in the Final, finding a way to breakdown the stubborn Germans when no one else could. Although he finished only second in the goal scoring charts, Pelé proved yet again that when it comes to all-round football talent, there's no one above him.

pulled it back for Tigana to fire in from the edge of the area. For all his skills Tigana scored only one goal in 49 internationals, so this was a pleasant surprise.

In the spell immediately before half-time Austria simply had to hold on. Last-ditch tackles seemed the order of the day: Happel on Fontaine and Hanappi to deny Platini. Ocwirk looked bemused and needed help. Memories of the 1954 mauling by West Germany (6-1) must have been prominent. Sindelar just wasn't strong enough to face this barrage and the two wingers were more whiz than wallop.

Meisl recognised the problem of course, and moved to address it at half-time. Obermayer was introduced to play sweeper with Koller and Hasil acting as wing-backs. Hanappi moved into midfield together with Prohaska, while Sindelar pushed further forward.

The changes did the trick. Almost immediately Hanappi dispossessed Kopa, and fed Sindelar, who's long-range lob nearly caught Barthez napping.

It turned out to be a false dawn for the Austrians however. Platini was enjoying himself, and quickly resumed the pressure. Juggling his way past Prohaska and Koller on the right, he crossed neatly, only for Fontaine to miss-time his header. Alain Giresse, on as a substitute, learnt his lines quickly. Receiving the ball from the back, he evaded Hanappi and duly fed Platini, who blasted a shot past Hiden's right hand post.

Austria were given a little hope with 15 minutes to go. Ocwirk finally got the ball to Sindelar, who sneaked past Jonquet and beat Barthez with a crisp shot.

France weren't to be denied though and both Papin and Giresse might have made it three before the end.

Austria exited with dignity in tact having surprised a few pundits. A couple of modern day champions might have made the difference, but the days when Austria produced greats like Binder, Sindelar and Ocwirk are sadly long gone.

France advanced to the quarter-finals happy in the knowledge that they had put on a stunning show in two of their three group games. That hammering by Germany, however, left an uneasy feeling, especially given the standard of competition to be faced in the knockout stages.

FRANCE: *Fabian Barthez; Lilian Thuram, Marcel Desailly, Robert Jonquet, Maxime Bossis; Jean Tigana (Alain Giresse 61), Didier Deschamps; Raymond Kopa, Michel Platini (Eric Cantona 89), Zinedine Zidane; Just Fontaine (Jean-Marie Papin 76)*
Subs not used: *Joel Bats, Manuel Amaros*
Goals: *Zidane 15, Tigana 23*

AUSTRIA: *Rudi Hiden; Gerhard Hanappi, Bruno Pezzey, Ernst Happel, Karl Koller; Franz Hasil, Ernst Ocwirk, Matthias Sindelar, Alfred Körner (Herbert Prohaska 45); Franz Binder (Erich Obermayer 45), Josef Bican (Hans Krankl 74)*
Subs not used: *Fritz Koncilia, Robert Sara*
Goal: *Sindelar 75*

GERMANY 3 SPAIN 1

Spain looked surprisingly committed as they faced the group's bully, eager to gain some redemption. Villalonga brought in Víctor Muñoz to help Guardiola in midfield, which kept the game relatively tight.

Germany, who weren't mathematically through to the next round, surprisingly rested a couple of players. Klinsmann and the East German Streich entered the fray, which was of little comfort to the Spanish.

As it was Spain coped well with Schuster and Overath, with Suarez finally looking something like the 1960 European Football of the Year. Gento didn't have any joy with Vogts, however. The German terrier made his living by taming the opposition's biggest dog.

The new German front line, was impressive. Rahn, back on the right, flew down the right wing, and drove a cross into the box. Klinsmann did well to get on to the end of it and Zamora did well if he even saw it. One-Nil.

Spain retained their composure, however. Suárez worked well with Michel on the right to carve an opening for Zarra, but Maier saved comfortably. Hierro decided to take matters into his own hand and drove forward, feeding Guardiola who hesitated for just long enough to allow Jürgen Kohler to step in.

Germany doubled their advantage with a sweet free kick by Overath after Rahn had again gone past Camacho.

half-time saw just one change, Müller coming on for Streich, although it would be a while before he got involved. Spain started the second period believing they could still get something from the game. Michel did well against Brehme and Suárez put a 20-foot shot past Maier. Almost immediately Gento had a chance to equalise. From Victor's pass he looked to be through on goal but strangely chose to pull it back for Raul, who was beaten out by the impressive Kohler.

Finally, Müller got into the action. Schuster guided one through the middle of Spain's defence and Müller was only foiled when Zamora stopped bravely at his feet. Germany were soon on the defensive again though. Camacho made his first real contribution, having his revenge of Rahn and crossing early before Vogts could get to him. Substitute Basora latched on to the deep ball and Maier was forced to save at the near post.

Spain couldn't catch a break. Overath miscued a pass aimed at Rahn, only for it to fall for Klinsmann, who outstripped Maceda and lined up Müller for his fourth of the tournament.

Spain finally conceded after that, but Germany were unable to capitalise. Overath, Schuster and Brehme all missed good opportunities and Zamora saved from Klinsmann.

Spain were out and talk of an under-achieving side promptly resumed. The critics missed the point. Spain lost because they weren't good enough. Decent strength in depth, but not enough great players. Perhaps that's always been the problem? Zamora was a giant, Gento and Suárez decent enough, but the supporting cast was no match for that of Germany, France, or even Austria. At least Raul offers hope for the future.

As Germany advanced to face England, the jury was still out after a mixed bag of performances in the group stage. Some of the reserves had done well against Spain but Müller wouldn't be left out again.

GERMANY: *Sepp Maier; Berti Vogts, Jürgen Kohler, Franz Beckenbauer, Andreas Brehme (Karl-Heinz Schnellinger 75); Bernd Schuster (Fritz Walter 72), Lothar Matthäus, Wolfgang Overath; Helmut Rahn, Jürgen Klinsmann, Joachim Streich (Müller 45)*
Subs not used: *Jurgen Croy, Uwe Seeler*
Goals: *Klinsmann 24, Overath 31, Müller 68*

SPAIN: *Ricardo Zamora; Chendo, Fernando Hierro, Antonio Maceda, José Camacho; Michel (Estanislao Basora 71), Víctor Muñoz, Josep Guardiola, Luis Suárez, Francisco Gento (Rafael Gordillo 75); Zarra (Raul 50)*
Subs not used: *Antonio Ramallets, Sergi*
Goal: *Suárez 50*

GROUP TWO DETAILS AND RESULTS

	P	W	D	L	F	A	GD	Pts
GERMANY	3	2	1	0	8	4	4	7
FRANCE	3	2	0	1	7	5	2	6
AUSTRIA	3	0	2	1	3	4	-1	2
SPAIN	3	0	1	2	2	7	-5	1

Germany and France qualify for quarter-finals

THE ALL-TIME WORLD CUP

Results

Germany	1-1	Austria
France	3-0	Spain
Germany	4-2	France
Austria	1-1	Spain
Spain	1-3	Germany
France	2-1	Austria

Goal Scorers

Four goals: Gerd Müller (Germany)
Three goals: Just Fontaine (France)
One goal each: Wolfgang Overath, Jürgen Klinsmann, Franz Beckenbauer, Helmut Rahn (all Germany), Luis Suárez, Zarra (both Spain), Franz Binder, Josef Bican, Matthias Sindelar (all Austria), Michel Platini, Zinedine Zidane, Jean Tigana, Bixente Lizarazu (all France)

GROUP THREE:
Hungary, Italy, Scotland, Uruguay

Each of the teams in Group Three has a strong football heritage, but the four protagonists have surprisingly little common history.

Uruguay have faced Hungary once and clashed with Italy and Scotland twice each. In 1954 they hammered Scotland 7-0, which probably made the Scots grateful that they'd chosen not to take their place in the 1950 competition. Had they done so they'd have met the eventual champions in the first round. In 1986 Scotland did well to draw with Uruguay, one of the pre-tournament favourites, although the South Americans had been thrashed by Denmark in their previous match.

Hungary and Uruguay's only meeting came in the thriller of 1954. Varela and Puskas wouldn't miss the re-match.

In 1970, Uruguay and Italy played out a morbid 0-0 draw, emphasising that each country has a history of safety-first football. If both teams were true to form, the Group Three match was likely to follow the low-scoring pattern. A second round match in 1990 had also seen Italy keep a clean sheet. Several defenders who helped Italy to a 2-0 victory that day would feature in the All-Time Italian team.

Italy defeated Hungary to win the World Cup Final in 1938. For Italy it marked the end of a fruitful spell, while Hungary were just beginning to emerge as a dominant force.

By the time the sides met again in a 1978 group match, Italy were back on the rise and Hungary were in decline. The likes of Tardelli, Scirea, Zoff and Rossi disposed of the Hungarians 3-1.

Scotland have never encountered Italy or Hungary in the World Cup finals. The failure of the Scots to progress out of the group stages has limited the opportunities, as has their late arrival on the World Cup scene. It's difficult to speculate how Scotland might have done had they entered the three World Cups in the 1930s, but they'd at least have expected to get through round one. They played continental opposition on fifteen occasions from 1929 until the War and lost only twice, including a 3-0 defeat at the hands of Italy in 1931. All four Group Three teams would call on 1930s stars, so Alex James and Hughie Gallacher would be able to judge themselves against Italy's Giusseppe Meazza, Uruguayan Hector Scarone and Györgi Sárosi of Hungary.

Italy and Scotland did meet twice in qualifying matches for the 1966 World Cup. Each won its home match, but it was Italy that progressed to the finals

101

where they'd lose a shocker to North Korea.

It was clear that this group would be one of the toughest to qualify from. Italy were favourites, of course, but Uruguay and Hungary looked well matched, and the Scots didn't have to worry about their usual folly of tripping over a minnow.

HUNGARY 3 SCOTLAND 0

Stein feared the worst and selected Billy Bremner in midfield, hopeful that the talented Hungarians wouldn't have the stomach for a fight.

From the start, the plan looked ill-advised. Bremner almost immediately gave the ball away and Hungary were in command. Bozsik fed Bene on the right who cut inside Caldow and teed one up for Puskas from 10 yards. "The Little Cannon" - as the Spanish called him - fired home without hesitation.

The Scots were already chasing the game, but without Alex James they were ill prepared for the task. Souness and Bremner charged around but couldn't catch up with the ball as it sped from one red shirt to another. It was soon 2-0. Czibor went down the left, but was well tackled by McGrain who forced the corner. From Albert's kick Mészöly nodded down for Kocsis to force it home.

Scotland were entrenched in their own half, under constant pressure. Kocsis might have added a third after he rose above Hansen, and Puskas manipulated the ball past Young to force a save from Goram. Bozsik, in particular, was in his element, drawing in a marker before whisking the ball away and supplying a team mate with an inch perfect pass.

As half-time approached Scotland finally bared their teeth. Souness split the defence with a long ball, but Matrai foiled Dalglish as he was poised to shoot.

At the interval Stein moved to address the situation. James was introduced for Johnstone who'd touched the ball precisely once. Jim Baxter came on for Morton, which left the Scots winger-less - but what point was there to wide men if you couldn't win or keep the ball?

The substitutes made an immediate impact. Baxter used his famous left foot to find James on the right. A quick jink and he set Law free. Grosics did well to turn the shot away. Souness connected well after the clearance from the corner, but rattled the woodwork.

Hopes of a Scottish comeback were soon put to rest. Kocsis held the ball up well on the edge of the area before Albert came flying through the middle, swerved past Young and easily beat Goram.

With 20 minutes to go, Dalglish showed his hand with a neat turn, but the shot didn't match the footwork and Grocsis was untroubled. James looked the best of the Scots, matching Bozsik for poise, but Law was isolated up front. The

THE MATCHES

Hungarians by contrast attacked in waves. Bene, Albert, Kocsis and Puskas all contributed to a fine move before the end. Czibor wasted the opportunity, blazing his shot wide.

Hungary had set the stage. It looked as if no defence could hold them, although the Italians would test that theory in the next match. For Scotland, only despair. For all the talent, they'd never really been in it. Stein needed to find a way to get his much-vaunted front pair into the game. At least wee Alex James wouldn't be on the bench next time.

HUNGARY: *Gyula Grosics; Jenö Buzánszky, Sándor Matrai, Kálmán Mészöly, Sándor Biró; Ferenc Bene, József Bozsik, Florian Albert (Györgi Sárosi 85), Zoltán Czibor; Ferenc Puskas, Sándor Kocsis (Ladislav Kubala 80)*
Subs not used: *Antal Szabó, Laszlo Balint, Lajos Detari*
Goals: *Puskas 6, Kocsis 18, Albert 60*

SCOTLAND: *Andy Goram; Danny McGrain, George Young, Alan Hansen, Eric Caldow; Jimmy Jonhstone (Alex James 45), Billy Bremner, Graeme Souness, Alan Morton (Jim Baxter 45) ; Kenny Dalglish, Denis Law (Hughie Gallacher 82)*
Subs not used: *Jim Brown, Dave McKay*

ITALY 0 URUGUAY 0

No prizes for predicting this one. Two of the strongest defences in the tournament faced off, and both seemed happy with the draw.

Uruguay withdrew Varela into defence where he duelled with Piola, while Santamaria went to work on Baggio. For Italy, Bergomi stuck close to Schiaffino and Collovati took care of Miguez. In midfield the tackles were flying. For all the talent possessed by Rocha, Rivera and Meazaa, none could find room to operate as Andrade, Benetti and Tardelli imposed themselves.

The Italians looked particularly robust. If England's midfield had set the standard for aggression, Tardelli and Benetti raised the bar another notch.

The first half saw just three shots on goal. First, Tardelli attacked down the right and put over a looping cross. Piola created a diversion and Meazza hit a crisp volley straight at the keeper. Schiaffino, frustrated by his close companion, dropped deep to supply a long pass to Andrade, who brushed off Benetti (really!) and tested the great Zoff from 20 yards.

The best chance fell to Maldini. With Cubilla safely in his pocket he advanced down the left, cut inside Victor Rodríguez Andrade, and exchanged passes with Baggio. Mazurkiewicz came out to meet him and forced Maldini to

103

hurry his shot, which crashed safely into the side netting.

Schiaffino was the liveliest of the playmakers, but Meazza was trying too. Rocha and Rivera were total bystanders.

Shortly after half-time Pozzo brought on Mazzola for Rivera, hopeful that an injection of poise would do the trick. Uruguay had a similar idea, and Scarone took an overdue bow.

It was the defenders who looked most dangerous coming forward, however. Varela charged by Meazza (or through him actually) and found his right-winger, but Cubilla couldn't get around the imperious Maldini.

Baresi, happy that his defence was in control, sauntered up field, starting a move that Piola might have finished after good work from Meazza.

The tackles continued to fly in midfield, and if Italy's artillery looked the heavier, it wasn't by much.

Antognoni and Francescoli, great talents from the 1980s, came on as substitutes, and both soon disappeared in the fracas.

A scoreless draw was fair enough and although there'd be prettier games than this, both sides had shown glimpses of what they might do going forward.

Uruguay would probably come out of their shell a little against Scotland, but Hungary could expect more of the same from Italy.

ITALY: *Dino Zoff; Giuseppe Bergomi, Franco Baresi, Fulvio Collovati, Paolo Maldini; Marco Tardelli, Romeo Benetti; Gianni Rivera (Sandro Mazzola 52), Giuseppe Meazza (Giancarlo Antognoni 73); Silvio Piola, Roberto Baggio (Luigi Riva 84)*
Subs not used: *Giampiero Combi, Giacinto Facchetti*

URUGUAY: *Ladislao Mazurkiewicz; Víctor Rodríguez Andrade, José Santamaría, José Nasazzi, Obdulio Varela, Alfonso Pereyra (Shubert Gambetta 80); José Leandro Andrade, Pedro Rocha (Hector Scarone 50); Luis Cubilla, Oscar Omar Míguez (Enzo Francescoli 71), Juan Schiaffino*
Subs not used: *Andrés Mazali, Fernando Morena*

URUGUAY 2 SCOTLAND 1

Scarone and James both started, bringing together two of the great pre-war inside forwards. Neither team had scored in their first match, so the infusion of playmaking skills was most welcome.

Stein was still tinkering with his line-up, also starting Baxter, although it seemed strange to leave out a fighter like Bremner just as the Uruguay heavies arrived on the scene.

Uruguay started brightly. Schiaffino, the instigator of most things good, set Scarone free on the right where he exchanged passes with Cubilla before putting a dangerous ball into the box. Young beat Míguez to it, but only just. Schiaffino was soon at it again. This time his through ball was well met by Cubilla, but the shot flew just wide. A third Uruguayan chance went begging before Scotland finally came out to play. James started the revival, jinking past Andrade and

Obdulio Varela

Obdulio Varela will forever be associated with the deciding game of the 1950 World Cup. Facing Brazil, the hosts and heavy favourites, Uruguay needed to win but when they went a goal down, all seemed bleak. Varela, one of the great captains, picked the ball out of the back of the net, walked back to the centre circle and then delayed the restart, supposedly arguing with the referee, all in a successful ploy to allow time for the crowd to calm down and for Brazil to lose their momentum.

Varela then began to assert himself on the match, starting the move that led to the equaliser. Uruguay won the game and the Cup in a huge upset. It seemed that Uruguay, and Varela, simply didn't know how to lose in World Cups. Four years later, they finally fell to Hungary, but significantly Varela didn't play in that game, and was never on the losing side in a World Cup match.

Varela made his club debut with Wanderers in 1938 and had already made his international bow by the time he joined Uruguayan giants Penarol in 1942.

An attacking centre-half, Varela created numerous goals and scored a fair few himself. Attacking centre-halves were a dying breed - Varela and Ernst Ocwirk were the last of their kind. But if Varela's position is now a relic, his skills transcend the eras. No player with that combination of skill, strength and unshakeable nerve can ever become out-dated. Varela often moved back into defence to help with potent centre-forwards before suddenly re-igniting the attack with a forceful run.

Varela retired after the 1954 World Cup having won 49 caps and scored 10 goals over a 15-year period. His retirement left a huge void in the national team and coincided with the decline of Uruguayan football. Perhaps one day, Uruguay will recover its status as a major footballing power, but it is unlikely that it will ever again see a player as dominant as Obdulio Varela.

supplying Law with an inch-perfect ball. A first-time shot was well hit, but Mazurkiewicz was equal to it.

Dalglish had the next chance. He coolly evaded Varela, and was poised for a shot when Nassazi came over to clear up the mess. Varela wasn't amused by his own lapse and so attempted to make amends. A strong run through the middle was ended only when Souness took him down from behind. Scarone struck the free kick, which curled in as Goram was left standing.

A goal down, Scotland urgently needed inspiration and received it immediately following the break. Baxter was not comfortable around Andrade, so switched to attack Uruguay's suspect left flank. A neat flick over Pereyra freed Johnstone who pulled back for Law to score neatly at the near post.

For a while, a Scottish win looked a real possibility. James came close with a lob, and McGrain had a thumping shot saved by the keeper.

With just two minutes to go, substitute Alcide Ghiggia broke Scotland's heart with an inspired winner. He worked his way past Baxter and Caldow before moving inside and shooting under the forlorn Goram. The hero of 1950 was at it again.

For once the Scots didn't deserve their plight. They'd matched the two-time World Cup winners for most of the match and had looked far more composed than against Hungary.

It was hard to see what the problem was. The goalkeeping could have been better, but Goram couldn't really be blamed for either goal. Perhaps the real difference between the sides was in expectations. In seven World Cup finals tournaments Scotland has only once beaten a major power - Holland in 1978. Although three of the All-Time Scottish side played in that match, the combined winning experience of the team pales in comparison with Uruguay, who had three World Cup winners sat on the bench.

A draw would be enough for Uruguay against Hungary, and the defence certainly looked up to the job.

Scotland would hope to sign off with a morale-boosting win over Italy, but would then go home, still having failed to do themselves justice in a World Cup.

URUGUAY: *Ladislao Mazurkiewicz; Victor Rodríguez Andrade, José Santamaría, José Nasazzi, Obdulio Varela, Alfonso Pereyra (Shubert Gambetta 74); José Leandro Andrade, Hector Scarone; Luis Cubilla (Alcide Ghiggia 78), Oscar Omar Míguez (Fernando Morena 77), Juan Schiaffino*
Subs not used: *Roque Máspoli, Pedro Rocha*
Goals: *Scarone 38, Ghiggia 88*

THE MATCHES

SCOTLAND: *Andy Goram; Danny McGrain, George Young, Alan Hansen (Billy McNeil 81), Eric Caldow; Alex James, Graeme Souness, Jim Baxter (Billy Bremner 70); Jimmy Johnstone, Denis Law, Kenny Dalglish (Hughie Gallacher 89)*
Subs not used: *Jim Brown, Billy Liddell*
Goal: *Law 50*

ITALY 2 HUNGARY 0

Italy sensed that for all the ball jugglers, Hungary were nothing special in defence. Pozzo ordered attack as the best means of defence, and as with most of Pozzo's plans, it worked to a tee.

Meazza took charge, slotting passes to his wing-backs who forced Czibor and Bene into unfamiliar territory. The first goal came after Maldini moved inside and sent Rivera away on the overlap. Bozsik was a magnificent player - smooth and controlled - but he was no intimidator, and Rivera had plenty of room to strut his stuff. Waltzing past Buzánszky he turned sharply towards goal and scored with a low shot which went in off the far post.

The Italians were in the mood and Baggio almost doubled the lead with a turn and volley. Meazza, Rivera and Baggio matched the Hungarians for skill, besides which their opposition was altogether less severe. Mészöly was masterful, so Piola stayed quiet, but the other defenders were all at sea. Scotland must have been sick to think that Law and Dalglish hadn't capitalised. The difference was in midfield. The Scots had been forever chasing shadows, but Bozsik and Albert couldn't escape Tardelli and Benetti in the same way.

When Puskas did finally get a decent pass, Bergomi and Baresi were there, swarming all around.

Kocsis remained a threat, even against big Collovati, but he was starved of the ball. Neither winger could break free, and Albert wasn't happy in midfield.

Sarosi's introduction helped a little, but the Italians smelled blood. After 70 minutes, Piola did well to hold off Mészöly, and Rossi - a surprise substitute - screeched in to kill the match. Puskas finally tricked Bergomi near the end, but Zoff was equal to his low shot.

After a brutal opening match, Italy had shown that the iron fist came with a velvet glove. Scotland were next, which looked like good news for Italy. Hungary now had to produce against Uruguay. Puskas and Kocsis needed to impose themselves, and there was every chance they would. But the defence had to hold firm too, and that looked altogether less likely.

Franco Baresi

Franco Baresi was the world's greatest defender for well over a decade, dominating the back line for both club and country. A mastermind in defence, Baresi was also dangerous in attack, launching and supporting attacks like no other defender since Beckenbauer.

It took a while for Baresi to displace Gaetano Scirea in the national team, but once he'd established himself, Baresi proved irreplaceable. In 1990, Italy boasted one of the greatest defences of all-time, and Baresi was the lynchpin. Probably the second best team in the competition, the Italians were unlucky to lose to Argentina on penalties in the semi-finals.

Four years later, Baresi and Italy were back and made it all the way to the Final, only to suffer another penalty shoot-out loss - this time to Brazil. After the first two group matches Baresi underwent knee surgery only to reappear in time for the Final!

In all, Baresi played in ten World Cup finals matches and was on the winning side seven times and lost only twice (discounting penalty defeats). With Baresi on duty Italy conceded only three goals in World Cup matches, a sign of the "Azzuri's" obsession with defence, but also a reflection of Baresi's greatness.

For all his success with the national team, Baresi was most famous for his role as captain of AC Milan. Milan dominated European football in the late 1980s and early 1990s. Gullit and Van Basten scored the goals, Baresi and Maldini helped prevent them. Between 1989 and 1995 Milan reached the European Cup Final five times and won three of them (although Baresi missed the 1994 Final through suspension). With Baresi at the helm, Milan also won three European Super Cups, two World Club Cups and five Italian League titles between 1988 and1996, as well as one back in 1979. Significantly, Milan kept a clean sheet in the Final each time they won a World Club or European Cup.

Baresi had joined Milan in 1974, a week after being rejected by great rivals Inter Milan, who had signed his elder brother Giuseppe. Franco turned professional three years later and made his international debut in 1982. Baresi won 81 caps in all, and by the time he retired in 1997, he was one of the most successful players of the modern era.

THE MATCHES

ITALY: *Dino Zoff; Giuseppe Bergomi, Franco Baresi, Fulvio Collovati; Marco Tardelli, Romeo Benetti, Gianni Rivera (Sandro Mazzola 82), Giuseppe Meazza, Paolo Maldini (Giacinto Facchetti 76); Silvio Piola, Roberto Baggio (Paolo Rossi 66)*
Subs not used: *Giampiero Combi, Giancarlo Antognoni*
Goals: *Rivera 26, Rossi 70*

HUNGARY: *Gyula Grosics; Jenö Buzánszky, Sándor Matrai (Gyula Lóránt 65), Kálmán Mészöly, Sándor Biró; Ferenc Bene (Ladislav Kubala 71), József Bozsik, Florian Albert (Görgi Sárosi 85), Zoltán Czibor; Ferenc Puskas, Sándor Kocsis*
Subs not used: *Antal Szabó, Lajos Detari*

ITALY 1 SCOTLAND 1

Italy weren't technically safe, but made a few changes anyway - although Facchetti, Mazzola, Antognoni and Rossi weren't exactly liabilities. For Scotland, Stein was still tinkering, this time trying Billy Liddle alongside Law and Dalglish and introducing Dave McKay in a reshuffled defence.

Scotland looked the hungrier with Souness and Bremner finally building a platform from which James and Dalglish could build. Liddle made the first chance, taking James' pass and going past Tardelli. Scirea cleared a high cross before Souness demanded a good save from Zoff. Benetti crunched Souness, as if to send a warning, but the Scott simply crunched him back and released Law through the middle. Bergomi's tackle was well timed and Scirea cleared the lines.

Mazzola was eager to keep his place in the side and started to show his skills. An intelligent player, he was soon creating dangerous openings - first for Tardelli and then for Antognoni.

The half ended with a snaking run from James that deserved better than his scuffed shot.

After the break, Italy struck. Facchetti, looking more like an all-time great than a reserve, marched down the left, beat Young and fired in a cross-shot. Goram bundled the ball out for a corner. Facchetti took it quickly and Rossi took advantage of the disorganised defence.

Although Dalglish had looked better in this tournament than in his previous three, he was quiet here. Stein took the opportunity to introduce Hughie Gallacher for his first prolonged outing. Immediately he made an impact. McGrain crossed from the right and Gallacher rose above Collovati to score. Perhaps the Italian defender didn't see the danger from Gallacher, who stood just

5'5, but the centre-forward scored numerous goals with his head.

Alan Morton came on with 20 minutes to go, and three "Wembley Wizards" (Morton, James and Gallacher) were reunited. Their understanding soon came in handy. Morton motored down the left, interchanged with James before crossing for Gallacher. Again Collovati was found wanting in the air, but Zoff was not.

The game lost momentum near the end, although Riva, making his second appearance of the competition, came close after beating McKay for pace.

Italy were through to meet France and must have been feeling confident. The likes of Law, Schiaffino and Puskas had managed just one goal between them.

Scotland were out, but had at least looked in the game this time, and created several goal chances. Still, in three matches they'd scored just twice. It seemed a poor return from a side boasting Britain's two finest strikers, but then neither Law nor Dalglish had ever brought Scotland much success in World Cups.

ITALY: *Dino Zoff; Giuseppe Bergomi, Gaetano Scirea, Fulvio Collovati, Giacinto Facchetti; Marco Tardelli, Romeo Benetti, Sandro Mazzola, Giancarlo Antognoni; Silvio Piola, Paolo Rossi (Luigi Riva 78)*
Subs not used: *Giampiero Combi, Paolo Maldini, Gianni Rivera, Franco Baresi*
Goal: *Rossi 48*

SCOTLAND: *Andy Goram; George Young, Alan Hansen, Dave McKay, Danny McGrain; Alex James, Graeme Souness, Billy Bremner; Denis Law, Kenny Dalglish (Hughie Gallacher 54), Billy Liddle (Alan Morton 71)*
Subs not used: *Jim Brown, Billy McNeil, Jim Baxter*
Goal: *Gallacher 57*

URUGUAY 1 HUNGARY 1

Finally Puskas and Varela would face off, although the Uruguayan actually gave most of his attention to Kocsis and left Puskas to Santamaria, a colleague of the Hungarian at Real Madrid.

Hungary needed the win and attacked with a controlled vengeance. Only Brazil had looked as fluid in attack as Hungary had against Scotland, but the defeat by Italy reminded them that they needed to mind their own net too. Puskas took centre stage, abusing Santamaria as he conjured two good chances. First, he turned inside and hit the post with the outside of his left boot. Then he took a high pass from Albert and coolly popped it up over Santamaria before hitting a volley straight at the keeper. Bene saw a rasping effort go wide before Albert's long-range effort hit the bar.

110

Uruguay were under siege, but soon reminded Hungary that they had attacking options of their own. Ghiggia skinned Biró and crossed for Míguez who nodded sharply down. Grosics did well to save, but Schiaffino was there to give Uruguay a precious lead.

Buoyed by the goal, the two Andrades and Varela began to assert their authority. Bozsik was a shadow of the smooth operator who'd pulled the strings against Scotland and Albert, who looked for a while something like the 1960s great, was brought under control.

Puskas, of course, wouldn't go quietly and shot just over from a free kick. The Hungarian captain kept trying and after an hour sent Bene away down the right. A deep cross was met in convincing fashion by the sound head of Kocsis, and Hungary were level. As Hungary poured forward they became more vulnerable to the break. Ghiggia might have punished them when he outpaced Matrai, but Grosics saved the day.

With 10 minutes left, Czibor launched a final desperate attack. His low ball was met first time by Albert but the impressive Mazurkiewicz saved with his feet. Puskas slapped the loose ball straight at Nassazi who cleared off the line.

Uruguay held on, and Hungary were sent to another crushing exit. It was easy to blame the defence, but Hungary had scored only once in their last two games. Puskas and Kocsis had met some outstanding defenders, and following the example of West Germany in 1954, Italy and Uruguay had refused to be intimidated.

Uruguay would get another chance to show their defensive prowess in the quarter-final, where they'd meet Brazil. No one could begrudge Uruguay their place, and they'd surely make a game of it, but it wouldn't be the same as watching Puskas versus Pelé.

URUGUAY: *Ladislao Mazurkiewicz; Victor Rodríguez Andrade, José Santamaría, José Nasazzi, Obdulio Varela, Shubert Gambetta; José Leandro Andrade, Hector Scarone (Pedro Rocha 75); Alcide Ghiggia (Luis Cubilla 88), Oscar Omar Míguez (Fernando Morena 88), Juan Schiaffino*
Subs not used: *Andrés Mazali, William Martinez*
Goal: *Schiaffino 34*

HUNGARY: *Gyula Grosics; Jenö Buzánszky, Sándor Matrai, Kálmán Mészöly, Sándor Biró; Ferenc Bene, József Bozsik (Györgi Sárosi 70), Florian Albert (Ladislav Kubala 72), Zoltán Czibor; Ferenc Puskas, Sándor Kocsis*
Subs not used: *Antal Szabó, Laszlo Balint, Lajos Detari*
Goal: *Kocsis 64*

WORLD CUP QUARTER-FINAL 1954, LAUSANNE

HUNGARY 4 URUGUAY 2

The champions versus the favourites, defence versus attack, and great players on either side. It had all the credentials of a classic and it didn't disappoint.

Hungary were favourites, unbeaten in three years and scorers of 21 goals in three matches in the tournament so far. But Uruguay were a serious threat. Their World Cup record listed ten wins and one draw, including an easy defeat of a decent England side in the quarter-finals.

The only disappointment was that both sides were without their best player and captain. Varela and Puskas were injured, but there were still plenty of greats on show.

It started as many expected. Hungary took an early lead when Czibor fired home after a header from Kocsis. Puskas's replacement Palatás had a shot saved by Máspoli and Hidegkuti also missed a chance - Hungary were clearly on top. It was almost half-time when Schiaffino failed to convert his team's first decent chance.

Shortly after the break, Hidegkuti scored with a header after fine work down the right from Bozsik and Kocsis led to a cross from Budai.

Other teams had rolled over at this point, but that wasn't the Uruguayan way. If Hungary thrived on magnificent passing movements, Uruguay's foundation was an exceptional defence spiced with some real individual flair and a strong will to win. They certainly missed Varela, and the useful Omar Míguez, but they still had Schiaffino and so were in with a shout. It was the great inside-forward who brought them back into it. A through-ball from Schiaffino was seized upon by Hohberg who held off a challenge to score. Another beautiful move from Schiaffino preceded another perfect through ball. Hohberg needed two attempts at it, but after Grocsis saved the first, the Míguez replacement converted for his second goal.

Uruguay were back in it, and Hungary looked under pressure for the first time in an age. Lórant had already twice cleared off the line and the South Americans had a deep belief that they should win World Cup matches.

Uruguay had the first chance in extra time, Hohberg this time hit the post and Schiaffino couldn't finish from the rebound. Worse still for the champions, Schiaffino, as well as right-half Rodríguez Andrade, were struggling with injury.

In the second period of extra time, Kocsis connected with a Budai cross to give Hungary the lead and then settled it for good with another header from Bozsik's delivery.

Uruguay were out and their era of domination was over. Few knew that Hungary's run was about to end too, upset by West Germany in the Final.

For all the famous matches played by the "Magic Magyars" this was probably the best. Against the strongest possible opposition, and without their leading man, they stood their ground for a fine victory in an exceptional match.

GROUP THREE DETAILS AND RESULTS

	P	W	D	L	F	A	GD	Pts
ITALY	3	1	2	0	3	1	2	5
URUGUAY	3	1	2	0	3	2	1	5
HUNGARY	3	1	1	1	4	3	1	4
SCOTLAND	3	0	1	2	2	6	-4	1

Italy and Uruguay qualify for quarter-finals

Results

Italy	0-0	Uruguay
Hungary	3-0	Scotland
Italy	2-0	Hungary
Uruguay	2-1	Scotland
Hungary	1-1	Uruguay
Italy	1-1	Scotland

Goal Scorers

Two goals: Paolo Rossi (Italy), Sándor Kocsis (Hungary)
One goal each: Gianni Rivera (Italy), Ferenc Puskas, Florian Albert (both Hungary), Juan Schaiffino, Alcide Ghiggia, Hector Scarone (all Uruguay), Denis Law, Hughie Gallacher (both Scotland)

GROUP FOUR:
Argentina, Holland, Portugal, Russia

In terms of success in World Cups, Group Four was the weakest in the tournament. Although each of the four sides has produced numerous quality players, only Argentina has ever fulfilled its potential.

Portugal have only participated in two finals tournaments, even failing to qualify in 1994 and 1998 when it could call upon several world class stars. Their World Cupqualification record is - along with Ireland's - easily the weakest of all the All-Time finalists.

Portugal have not met any of their Group Four rivals in the World Cup finals, although in 1966 they played the Soviet Union in the third-place play-off - a game Eusebio and co. won 2-1. That marked Portugal's best World Cup showing. They were eliminated in the first round in 1986 having beaten England in their first match.

Most of Russia's finals experience is tied up with that of the Soviet Union. Only in 1994 did Russia compete in its own right. They got off to an inauspicious start, exiting in round one. The Soviet Union was a little more successful. In seven finals appearances they made four quarter-finals, although they only advanced to the next stage in 1966. The Soviet Union also lost its only other match against Group Four opposition, 2-0 against Argentina in a 1990 group match.

Argentina's record over the last 20 years has been impressive and includes two Cups and a Final appearance in 1990. They were also runners-up in the first competition in 1930, but fell on lean times between then and 1978.

Argentina's successful spell has coincided with the revival of Dutch football, and they have met three times in World Cups. Most recently they lost 2-1 to Holland in the 1998 quarter-final. Holland would fall at the next hurdle, thus depriving them of the opportunity to win the trophy for the first time. On their previous trip to the Final in 1978, Argentina had again been the foe and the host country - inspired by Kempes - triumphed 3-1 in extra time. The Argentinian captain that day, Daniel Passarella, along with Fillol, Ardiles and Kempes, would start for the All-Time side, which would reunite them with Holland's Krol, Neeskens and Suurbier.

Holland were probably stronger in 1974 and crushed Argentina 4-0 in the second round, although they again lost in the Final, this time to West Germany.

THE MATCHES

HOLLAND 4 RUSSIA 0

Russia weren't expected to win, but a team with Yashin and Schesternev wasn't supposed to leak goals like this. They employed a man on each of Holland's three forwards with Khidiatulin sweeping up behind. The plan worked, at least for the first half.

Holland didn't start well. Cruyff was strangely quiet and while Van Hanegem launched plenty of attacks, they never seemed to reach fruition. Van Basten couldn't rid himself of Schesternev and Onopko did well against Gullit. He'd controlled the dread-locked star well in the European Championships in 1992 and clearly wasn't impressed by reputation.

Russia might have threatened in attack if Nesskens and Davids hadn't put such a firm hold on midfield. Ivanov showed sparks of the form that made him one of the best players in the inaugural European Championships, but there was little from Voronin or the famous Netto.

Rijkaard, on a run from the back, created the best chance, opening up the Russian defence only for Cruyff to scuff his shot.

After the break, everything changed. Perhaps Michels had a word, but whatever it was, Holland looked a different team. Khlestov had done relatively well with Cruyff, but now he looked out of his league. The Dutch talisman pulled him one way and then the other. He crossed with the outside of his right foot and Neeskens connected first time with a thunderbolt that even Yashin couldn't stop. Soon Cruyff was free again. This time he went inside his marker and around the covering Khidiatulin. Yashin came to meet him but Cruyff lifted his shot over the black wall to double the lead.

Only Ivanov and little Chislenko looked dangerous for Russia. Ivanov's pass and Chislenko's subsequent cross created their best - their only - chance, but Bobrov headed straight at the keeper.

Gullit was ready to join the action and moved into the middle. Suurbier filled the gap and crossed to the far post. Gullit's prodigious leap took him above Khidiatulin and Yashin was beaten again.

If some began to doubt Yashin's elevated status, it was a harsh judgement. He'd had no chance with any of the goals and made smart saves from Davids and Krol. Schesternev looked as good as promised; Van Basten hardly got a kick. But what did it matter if the rest of the defence collapsed around him?

Cruyff added the fourth near the end after good work from Van Hanegem, but by then the Dutch were back in cruise mode. They'd only really engaged for 30 minutes and won 4-0. It was doubtful that even Michels could get them to play at full throttle for an entire match, but on this evidence an hour in top gear would be more than enough.

Johan Neeskens

Probably the greatest ball winner to ever play the game, Johan Neeskens was an essential element in the great Ajax and Holland teams of the 1970s.

Neeskens' aggression and energy set the tone for the entire team and allowed Ajax to develop new tactics. The midfielder would chase down opponents - often the other team's main ball player - helping to introduce the art of "pressing". As David Winner explains it in his book Brilliant Orange: "Neeskens' prey tended to try to retreat into their own half to try and get away from him. Naturally, Neeskens chased after them..."

But Neeskens was more than just a terrier. Neeskens could run with the ball and had tremendous shooting power - which helped bring him 17 goals in 49 internationals. Quick and good in the air, there wasn't anything Neeskens couldn't do on a football field. His versatility enabled him to play in defence or attack, but it was in the middle where he could exert most influence.

Having started out with Harlem, Neeskens moved to Ajax in 1970. That was also the year he made his first international appearance at the age of 19. Four years later Neeskens would play a starring role in the drama that was the 1974 World Cup Final. Neeskens scored from the first penalty awarded in a World Cup Final after just two minutes - but Holland went on to lose the game.

Unlike Cruyff, Neeskens was back four years later, and suffered another heartbreaking loss in the Final.

Neeskens did find glory in club football, however. With Ajax, he won three consecutive European Cups and three Dutch League titles. At the end of the 1973-74 season he joined Cruyff and former Ajax coach Rinus Michels at Barcelona, where he won a Spanish Cup and the Cup-Winners Cup in 1979.

In 1981 Neeskens left Barcelona to play in the USA. Although he later tried a comeback in Switzerland, his top-flight career was over after over a decade flying high as the greatest midfielder in football.

THE MATCHES

HOLLAND: *Jan van Beveren; Wim Suurbier, Ronald Koeman, Frank Rijkaard, Ruud Krol; Edgar Davids (Wim Jansen 78), Johan Neeskens, Wim van Hanegem; Ruud Gullit, Marco van Basten (Dennis Bergkamp 80), Johan Cruyff*
Subs not used: *Edwin van der Sar, Frank de Boer, Rob Rensenbrink*
Goals: *Neeskens 49, Cruyff 56, 81, Gullit 68*

RUSSIA: *Lev Yashin; Vagiz Khidiatulin; Dmitri Khlestov, Albert Schesternev, Victor Onopko; Valery Voronin (Fyodor Cherenkov 69), Valentin Ivanov, Igor Netto; Igor Chislenko, Eduard Streltsov, Vsevolod Bobrov (Valeri Karpin 62)*
Subs not used: *Rinat Dasayev, Yuri Kovtun, Andrei Kanchelskis*

ARGENTINA 3 PORTUGAL 2

This was a fine match, although not as close as the scoreline suggests. Argentina were marvellous, crafting openings from the start and continuing to put on a show throughout. Portugal were lucky to get close.

Before the tournament there was a worry as to how Maradona and Di Stefano would combine. Both were used to being the focal point of their side's attack, which might have caused difficulties but in actuality simply made Argentina unstoppable. Di Stefano took on the role of midfield general, dictating the play and roaming from box to box with his famous energy. Meanwhile, Maradona operated in bursts of inspiration. Portugal were left bewildered.

It started after just three minutes. Ardiles made progress down the right and laid it off to Di Stefano, who swerved around Sousa and committed Couto before feeding Kempes with the perfect ball. Costa Pereira was stunned.

A goal down, Portugal attempted to find a rhythm but their playmakers received close attention. Marzolini stifled Figo and Monti patrolled the pastures in front of his defence in which Coluna preferred to operate.

After Batistuta nodded over from a free kick, Maradona made his first contribution. Starting from the centre circle, he broke forward, nipped past Sousa and drifted left where he sped by João Pinto. Maradona cut inside and as Germano advanced passed to Di Stefano who gratefully made it 2-0.

Portugal were desperate to get into the game and for a short while reverted to the long ball. Couto fired up a high floater that only Torres could ever reach. His knock-down fell to Coluna but the shot was blocked.

Di Stefano regained control and found Marzolini on the overlap. A high cross was met by Batistuta and Costa Pereira did well to push it behind. Germano cleared the corner as he attempted to restore order.

Before the interval, Torres gave Portugal some hope. Figo found enough room to cut inside and play it in to the big man. Torres used his strength to turn on Ruggeri and shoot past Fillol.

Rui Costa came on for Futre at half-time but he had no time to settle in - Maradona was at it again. Turning and twisting on the edge of the area, he finally squirmed past Dimas and curled his shot around the keeper. The Portugese defence was in position, but was powerless to stop the little maestro.

Figo drifted inside and at last began to look like a footballer, but Argentina were on a different level - at least for today. Even the hard men could play. One Figo run was abruptly ended by Monti, who quickly released Marzolini for another dangerous foray.

Periera's impressive display kept his side in it. Twice Di Stefano was denied, and Kempes looked certain to score before an astounding reflex stop.

As the clock wound down Portugal got a goal back. Spectators had probably forgotten that Eusebio was on the pitch. Starved of possession, and well marshalled by Passarella's crew, Portugal's most famous player had been consigned to the fringes. In the final minute he finally received the ball from Rui Costa. Ruggeri and Passarella could only watch as Eusebio sprinted through. Fillol didn't touch the high shot.

It was nice to see, but of little consolation to Portugal, who'd thought they were a match for Argentina. In the event, the South Americans had the edge in every department. Germano, Torres and Sousa all had good reputations, but Passarella, Batistuta and Monti looked better. And if Portugal thought that Figo and Eusebio would scare opponents, they hadn't seen Di Stefano and Maradona.

Yashin's Russia would be the next to try and stop Argentina's onslaught. Meanwhile, Portugal hoped that those who said Holland were actually the group's best team were just joking.

ARGENTINA: *Ubaldo Fillol; Jorge Olguin, Daniel Passarella, Oscar Ruggeri, Silvio Marzolini; Luis Monti (Antonio Rattin 80); Osvaldo Ardiles (Jorge Burruchaga 78), Alfredo Di Stefano, Diego Maradona; Mario Kempes (Juan Manuel Moreno 65), Gabriel Batistuta*
Subs not used: *Amedeo Carrizo, Roberto Perfumo*
Goals: *Batistuta 3, Di Stefano 15, Maradona 50*

PORTUGAL: *Alberto da Costa Pereira; João Domingos Silva Pinto, Fernando Couto, Germano, Manuel Dimas; Luis Figo, Paulo Sousa (Humberto Coelho 66), Mário Coluña, Paulo Futre (Rui Costa 45); Eusebio, José Torres (José Águas 76)*
Subs not used: *Victor Baia, José Augusto*
Goals: *Torres 41, Eusebio 90*

Alfredo Di Stefano

Before Pelé there was Alfredo, the star player and captain of the Real Madrid team that won five consecutive European Cups. Some observers still consider Alfredo Di Stefano the greatest player of all-time.

Certainly Di Stefano is the best never to have played in the World Cup finals (sorry Mr Best). That he didn't is partly due to injury. His adopted country of Spain qualified in 1962, and although Di Stefano was in the squad, he didn't play. It's pure speculation as to whether his presence would have helped the team - which already included Puskas, Gento and Suárez - progress beyond the first round, but by then Di Stefano and the other Real stars were past their best. Perhaps 1958 was the better shot, but a loss at rain-soaked Hampden to Scotland and a draw with Switzerland cost them a place in the finals. Despite the disappointments, Di Stefano still managed to score 23 goals for Spain in 31 appearances.

Of course, if today's rules had applied, Di Stefano would not have played for Spain at all.

Di Stefano was born near Buenos Aires in Argetnina and began playing for River Plate at the age of 18. He soon found his way into the national team, who he helped win the South American Championship in 1947. Two years later, however, a strike by Argentinian players, led to a lock-out by the clubs. Di Stefano and other top players from around the world (including England's Neil Franklin) joined a private league not recognised by FIFA in Colombia. Di Stefano played for Millionarios and also the Colombian national team.

On tour with his club in Spain, Di Stefano attracted the attentions of Spanish giants Barcelona and Real Madrid. Barcelona agreed to buy the centre-forward from River Plate, which was the last FIFA-recognised club that Di Stefano had represented. Real, meanwhile, came to a deal with Millionarios. It was eventually decided that the Argentine would play one season for each club, but after failing to impress in early matches for Real, Barcelona conceded their rights.

Di Stefano's all around talent soon transformed Real into the greatest club side in the world, and even though the club could also call on the talents of Puskas, Gento and Raymond Kopa, there was no doubt that the Argentinian was the main man.

Di Stefano combined magnificent ball skills with tremendous energy and understanding of the game. He dictated play from midfield, but was not a static general. He roamed all over the pitch and as well as laying on countless chances for his team mates, he scored many goals himself. He was on the score sheet in each of first the five European Cup Finals, including a hat trick in 1960. He topped the Spanish scoring charts five times between 1954 and 1959 and scored 49 goals in 58 matches in the European Cup.

Di Stefano wasn't always one of the most popular personalities off the pitch, but his on-field heroics ensure him a place at the apex of the footballing pyramid.

ARGENTINA 3 RUSSIA 1

Argentina killed Russian hopes quickly before easing off the throttle in the second half. Di Stefano was again the driving force, running past and around his markers before feeding the hungry strikers.

Kempes scored the first from Di Stefano's pass. Yashin got a finger to it, but couldn't stop it rolling in off the post. Maradona was shadowed by Oleg

Dolmatov, a specialist man-marker who'd once kept George Best quiet in a European Championship game. He didn't have the same luck here. Maradona went deep to get the ball and then attacked. Dolmatov was right there but couldn't quite get in the challenge. It reminded observers of 1986 when Peter Reid had chugged behind the great man as he waltzed towards that wonder goal against England. This time, after Netto and Voronin had also missed him, Schesternev came across, but the ball squirmed free to Batistuta who made no mistake from 10 yards.

Di Stefano had a couple of long-range efforts that brought good saves from Yashin, and Ardiles supplied a neat back-healed pass for Monti, who might have done better with his shot. Again the Russian playmakers looked timid. Monti, the only defence-minded Argentine midfielder, might have struggled had Netto, Ivanov and Voronin summoned the courage to challenge him. As it was, the forwards had to do their own dirty work. Streltsov - who was highly skilled - came deep and ran past Monti and Ruggeri before feeding Chislenko, who should have at least hit the target.

Argentina sealed the win early in the second period. Passarella charged up field and played in Marzolini who deceived Yashin and scored with a reverse shot to the left. After the goal Menotti brought on his substitutes and Argentina lost some momentum.

Netto finally remembered how to pass and found Streltsov with a through ball. A quick swerve around Passarella preceded a firm shot past Fillol.

Russia had hope, but the fightback never gained momentum. Two games and seven goals conceded. It didn't look good for Yashin's men, but the opposition was pretty good. Argentina were already through and could now look forward to a showdown with Holland.

ARGENTINA: *Ubaldo Fillol; Jorge Olguin, Daniel Passarella, Oscar Ruggeri, Silvio Marzolini; Luis Monti (Antonio Rattin 60); Osvaldo Ardiles (Jorge Burruchaga 64), Alfredo Di Stefano, Diego Maradona; Mario Kempes (Juan Manuel Moreno 60), Gabriel Batistuta*
Subs not used: *Amedeo Carrizo, Roberto Perfumo*
Goals: *Kempes 13, Batistuta 21, Marzolini 51*

RUSSIA: *Lev Yashin; Vagiz Khidiatulin; Oleg Dolmatov, Albert Schesternev, Victor Onopko; Valery Voronin (Valeri Karpin 60), Valentin Ivanov, Igor Netto; Igor Chislenko, Eduard Streltsov, Vsevolod Bobrov*
Subs not used: *Rinat Dasayev, Yuri Kovtun, Andrei Kanchelskis, Fyodor Cherenkov*
Goal: *Streltsov 72*

HOLLAND 2 PORTUGAL 2

Holland were again slow into their running and suffered the consequences.

Michels, aware that Torres was a handful, introduced Barry Hulshoff and pushed Rijkaard into midfield. Hulshoff - always excellent in the air - handled the Portugese giant well, but Eusebio was left unmarked and made the Dutch pay.

After Coluña had tested Van Beveren with an early lob, Portugal struck. Rui Costa supplied a neat pass and Eusebio ran straight by Koeman and beat the keeper with a heavy blow. Perhaps this Portugese side was something special after all?

Eusebio certainly seemed to think so and added his second after just 20 minutes. This time he attacked from the left flank, exchanged passes with Coluña and struck another rocket past Van Beveren.

Michels and Cruyff looked bemused, but soon went about rectifying the problem in their own separate ways. The coach brought on Frank de Boer to shadow Eusebio while Cruyff sought to take over the game. Moving through the middle he found Gullit who shrugged off Dimas and created an easy goal for Van Basten.

Neeskens asserted himself in midfield and, confident that Rijkaard would cover him, moved forward. One rasping effort shook the bar; the next was just wide. Cruyff continued to push forward. He beat João Pinto on the left and cut inside, but Germano beat Van Basten to the pass. Another Dutch goal seemed inevitable, but Portugal held firm. Germano was a great player and even Van Basten couldn't exploit him. The full-backs were over matched against Gullit and Cruyff but somehow hung on.

When they got the ball Portugal retained possession well. Figo, Coluña and Rui Costa stroked it about beautifully, but sooner or later Rijkaard or Neeskens stepped in and another Dutch attack was underway. It was Rijkaard who finally crafted the equaliser. With time running out, he brushed off Rui Costa and hit a cross-shot that Couto deflected straight to Cruyff.

It was hard on Portugal, but they'd been at breaking point for an hour, and Holland worked hard for their draw. Portugal needed to win their final game and hope that Argentina beat Holland. Eusebio's team couldn't be counted out, but it was unlikely that Holland would be so sloppy two games in row.

THE ALL-TIME WORLD CUP

HOLLAND: *Jan van Beveren; Wim Suurbier, Ronald Koeman, Barry Hulshoff, Ruud Krol; Frank Rijkaard, Johan Neeskens, Wim van Hanegem (Frank de Boer 27); Ruud Gullit (Rob Rensenbrink 77), Marco van Basten (Dennis Bergkamp 77), Johan Cruyff*
Subs not used: *Edwin van der Sar, Edgar Davids*
Goals: *Van Basten 30, Cruyff 87*

PORTUGAL: *Alberto da Costa Pereira; João Domingos Silva Pinto, Fernando Couto, Germano, Dimas; Luis Figo, Paulo Sousa, Mário Coluña, Rui Costa (Humberto Coelho 75) ; Eusebio, José Torres (José Augusto 84)*
Subs not used: *Victor Baía, José Águas, Paulo Futre*

PORTUGAL 2 RUSSIA 2

If Argentina beat Holland, Portugal could still qualify with a win over Russia, who were playing only for pride.

Portugal generally had the upper hand although Russia made a game of it. Schesternev, again looked excellent, easily dealing with Torres, but Eusebio remained a menace. After a Russian attack broke down, Coluña found his Benfica team mate with a long pass, and Eusebio held off his marker and shot past Yashin. In 1966 Eusebio had scored his ninth goal of the tournament from the penalty spot against Yashin in the third-place playoff.

Russia were soon back in it, however. Ivanov and Netto combined neatly in midfield to give Streltsov half a chance. He still had Couto to beat when he received the ball, but made light work of the sweeper and easily beat Costa Pereira. Had Russia got him the ball in the first two matches, who knows what might have happened?

At least he got a chance to shine here. Costa Pereira was forced into a great save after Streltsov volleyed coolly from a corner.

Portugal regained the lead with a sublime goal, made by Figo. The Portugese winger had looked decent enough in the earlier matches but hadn't really imposed himself. Starting on the right he went outside and then moved inside Netto and swerved past Khidiatulin. Only Yashin stood in his way, and he might have converted himself, but instead fed Eusebio for his fifth of the competition.

Russia's neat passing was pre-eminent in the second half, but Germano stood in the way and it was injury time before Russia grabbed a deserved equaliser.

Ivanov surged down the right and was about to shoot when Chislenko took it off him and hit home from the edge of the area.

Russia at least avoided humiliation, but Yashin, Schesternev and Streltsov could have done with some help. Great Soviet players like Blokhin and

Kuznetsov might have made a difference.

Portugal had impressed in patches but were unlucky to meet two exceptional sides. At least Eusebio got to score a few, but that was little consolation for Portugal, who perhaps paid the price for their World Cup inexperience.

PORTUGAL: *Alberto da Costa Pereira; João Domingos Silva Pinto, Fernando Couto, Germano, Manuel Dimas; Luis Figo, Paulo Sousa, Mário Coluña, Rui Costa (Chalana 85); Eusebio, José Torres (José Águas 65)*
Subs not used: *Victor Baía, José Augusto, Humberto Coelho*
Goals: *Eusebio 25, 41*

RUSSIA: *Lev Yashin; Vagiz Khidiatulin; Andrei Kanchelskis, Albert Schesternev, Victor Onopko; Valery Voronin, Valentin Ivanov, Igor Netto; Igor Chislenko, Eduard Streltsov, Vsevolod Bobrov (Valeri Karpin 50)*
Subs not used: *Rinat Dasayev, Fyodor Cherenkov, Dmitri Khlestov, Igor Shalimov*
Goals: *Strelsov 35, Chislenko 92*

HOLLAND 4 ARGENTINA 3

This was the best match of the tournament. Both sides looked to attack and both had plenty of artillery. Holland needed a result to be safe and were more urgent in their approach, moving quickly with and without the ball. Over the years Holland have won countless fans for their displays of high skill at speed - something no other country has ever really matched. Argentina were impressive too, but their style was altogether different. Like most South American teams they played at a slower pace before a bit of individual magic set the game alight.

Neeskens dictated the tempo, tearing around the pitch, harassing Argentina's ball players into mistakes. Monti made his acquaintance, of course, but not even that giant could intimidate Neeskens. Cruyff again looked sharp - and sped by Olguin and Ruggeri to force a save from Fillol - before creating the opener for Van Basten. After a quiet start to the tournament, the tall striker was in the mood. The crisp volley from Cruyff's cross had quality written all over it.

For all the dynamism, Dutch teams have a habit of giving opponents a chance to recover. Argentina didn't need asking twice. Davids had close tabs on Di Stefano, but the Real Madrid legend seemed undeterred. He moved forward before suddenly putting on the brakes. Davids ran straight past him and Di Stefano had time to feed Burruchaga who forced the ball into the box. Kempes was there first, and it was all-square.

The reprieve was short-lived. Cruyff - rising to Di Stefano's level - broke through the middle and crashed a shot against the post. Van Basten poked in the rebound.

It was level again before the break. Maradona, carefully followed by Suurbier, finally wriggled free and floated a teaser into the box. Van Beveren didn't commit and Batistuta had time to control on his chest before lashing home. Argentina's strikers were scoring for fun in this tournament, but there'd been plenty of easy pickings.

Holland went for broke after the break. Bergkamp was introduced in place of Van Hanegem, who'd suffered under Monti's microscope. Bergkamp soon made the difference, sprinting past Monti to provide Van Basten with a chance for his hat-trick. From a tight angle he shot high and hard. Fillol knocked it safely over for a corner.

Van Basten quickly made amends, blasting in from the right after another Bergkamp pass.

Argentina weren't finished though. Marzolini, who'd done a good job on Gullit, attacked down the left before Maradona took over. A swerve inside saw him brought down by Koeman. A penalty was the only possibility and Di Stefano converted from the spot.

Some of the Holland players might have thought about settling for the draw, but not Neeskens. A neat pass from Cruyff set his midfield partner free through the middle and a heavy Neeskens shot made Fillol an irrelevance.

Holland had won the shoot-out, but it was clear that both of these sides were a threat. The result meant that Holland would top the group and face France in the quarters. For Argentina it would be Italy. Neither was an easy assignment, but Holland were probably the happier.

HOLLAND: *Jan van Beveren; Wim Suurbier, Ronald Koeman, Frank Rijkaard, Ruud Krol; Edgar Davids, Johan Neeskens, Wim van Hanegem (Dennis Bergkamp 49); Ruud Gullit (Marc Overmars 84), Marco van Basten, Johann Cruyff*
Subs not used: *Edwin van der Sar, Wim Jansen, Rob Rensenbrink, Frank de Boer*
Goals: *Van Basten 20, 29, 60, Neeskens 81*

ARGENTINA: *Ubaldo Fillol; Jorge Olguin, Daniel Passarella, Oscar Ruggeri, Silvio Marzolini; Luis Monti (Antonio Rattin 76); Jorge Burruchaga (Osvaldo Ardiles 84), Alfredo Di Stefano, Diego Maradona; Mario Kempes, Gabriel Batistuta (Juan Manuel Moreno 82)*
Subs not used: *Amedeo Carrizo, Roberto Perfumo*
Goals: *Kempes 26, Batistuta 37, Di Stefano 71 (pen)*

WORLD CUP FINAL 1978, BUENOS AIRIES

ARGENTINA 3 HOLLAND 1

Two famous footballing nations were seeking to fulfil their World Cup destiny, but Argentina could call on home support and some co-operative refereeing to give fate a helping hand.

Holland progressed to the Final in reasonable order, recovering from a loss to Scotland to hammer Austria, hold West Germany, and squeeze past Italy in the Second Phase. That match against Italy might have made the best Final, but Argentina were on a mission.

They beat (and sometimes battered) Hungary and France, before losing to Italy in the first round, and progressed to the Final by holding Brazil and recording wins over Poland and Peru. They needed to win the last match by three and ran out 6-0 winners, which led to allegations that the fascist Argentinian government had bribed Peru.

Nonetheless, Argentina took their place in the Final and immediately caused trouble, insisting that René van de Keerkhof be excluded because of a cast on his arm. Dutch captain Ruud Krol claims he threatened to lead his team off, after which Van de Keerkhof was allowed to play, once he added an extra bandage.

Once underway, the game immediately turned nasty, Poortvliet and Haan got their retaliation in first with harsh tackles. Haan showed the other side of his game to provide Rep with a headed chance from a free kick after five minutes. There might have been several goals in the first half; Jongbloed saved from Bertoni after a Kempes pass, and Rep had a shot pushed over by the impressive Fillol.

Eventually, after 37 minutes, Kempes broke the deadlock. The deep-lying striker was Argentina's inspiration throughout the tournament, and he didn't let them down here. A move started by Ardiles saw Luque play the ball across the area. Kempes got to it first and slid his shot under Jongbloed. Rensenbrink might have equalised just before half-time, but this wasn't his day.

The Dutch attacked in the second half, but Argentina held out through a combination of fair and foul. The referee is widely and rightly blamed for not taking stronger action - but the Dutch were hardly saints themselves.

In the 82nd minute they earned a reprieve. Substitute Nanninga headed in after the useful Van der Kerrkhof crossed.

Holland almost won it in the final minute. Rensenbrink - Holland's player of the tournament - might have stolen the global spotlight had his shot, from a tight angle on the left, gone in rather than hit the post.

As it was, extra time was needed and Kempes re-imposed himself.

After a goalmouth panic, which initially saw Jongbloed save, Kempes pushed home the go-ahead goal. Argentina were within touching distance, and Kempes was in the mood. Charging through again he provided the assist for Bertoni, who fulfilled his own prophecy that he'd score in the Final as Argentina lifted the World Cup.

Many in Holland felt that the home crowd and a lenient referee meant they never stood a chance, but it would have helped if their best players had shown up. Neither Johan Cruyff or Wim van Hanegem were available, and the lustre seemed to be fading from Holland's golden period. The stars of Ajax were now dispersed around Europe and they even had a foreign coach - famous Austrian Ernst Happel. For Holland this was the end of an era. They didn't return to the finals for 12 years, by which time Argentina had again won the World Cup.

GROUP FOUR DETAILS AND RESULTS

	P	W	D	L	F	A	GD	Pts
HOLLAND	3	2	1	0	10	5	5	7
ARGENTINA	3	2	0	1	9	7	2	6
PORTUGAL	3	1	2	1	6	7	-1	2
RUSSIA	3	0	1	2	3	9	-6	1

Holland and Argentina for quarter-finals

Results

Holland	4-0	Russia
Argentina	3-2	Portugal
Holland	2-2	Portugal
Argentina	3-1	Russia
Holland	4-3	Argentina
Portugal	2-2	Russia

Goal Scorers

Five goals: Eusebio (Portugal)
Four goals: Van Basten (Holland)
Three goals: Batistuta (Argentina), Cruyff (Holland)
Two goals: Kempes, Di Stefano (both Argentina), Neeskens (Holland), Streltsov (Russia)
One goal each: Maradona, Marzolini (both Argentina), Gullit (Holland), Torres (Portugal), Chislenko (Russia)

Quarter-finals

BRAZIL 3 URUGUAY 1

Uruguay's defence had stood up to some fine forwards in the group matches - Piola, Law, and even Puskas had gotten little change from the Uruguayans - but nothing could have prepared them for Pelé in this form.

The great man had looked good, but not devastating, in his first matches. All that changed here. Every attack seemed to begin with a Pelé flick or feint. After just seven minutes he spun past Santamaria and shot fiercely at Mazurkiewicz. The keeper saved well, but notice had been served.

Pelé came from deep to create the opening goal. Using his famed strength to fend off Andrade he glided forward and picked his moment before setting Garrincha free on the right. Gambetta was out of position and Garrincha made straight for goal. Mazurkiewicz parried the shot but couldn't keep it out.

Pelé added the second almost immediately. Rivelino crossed from the left and Pelé connected with a flying header. Not even Banks could have saved that one. Brazil were on their way, but the defence looked shaky enough for Uruguay to believe they could come back.

Back in 1950, little Ghiggia was the key to the revival against a superior Brazilian team, but he didn't have the same impact here. Nílton Santos was on guard and coped well. It was left to Schiaffino to lead the way. He exchanged passes with Morena before letting fly with a shot that Gilmar did well to block. Only Scarone looked like giving him much help, but his bursts of inspiration rarely lasted long.

Pelé was back at it after half-time. He shot wide after bursting by Nassazi straight from the restart, but soon repeated his run and this time shot smoothly under Mazurkiewicz. At 3-0, the game was truly over. Varela picked the ball out of the net, but there were no delaying tactics this time, and no miracle comeback either.

Morena gave his team some hope when he volleyed home Gambetta's cross, and if Schiaffino's shot had gone in rather than hit the bar, perhaps Uruguay would have stood a chance.

Pelé, of course, had the final word. As Uruguay pushed forward, Pelé hit them on the break and lobbed the keeper from the centre circle - a move he patented over thirty years ago. As in 1970, the shot drifted wide to deny the master his hat-trick - but it really wasn't about the numbers.

Uruguay could have no complaints; they were simply blown away by the world's greatest player. Andrade and Varela had done well against Didi and Ademir but Brazil had still won easily as they sat back and let their favourite son do everybody's favourite thing.

Garrincha

One of the most magically gifted of all Brazilian players, Garrincha's achievements were all the more remarkable given that his legs were badly twisted from a childhood illness.

Garrincha was the last of the great outside rights, an all out attacking position that became defunct during the late 1960s as Garrincha's career wound down. Before then, "Little Bird" left the world with some fond memories, starring in two World Cup wins.

When Brazil arrived in Sweden in 1958, Garrincha - like Pelé - was not a regular in the team. After a couple of lack-lustre Brazilian performances, coach Vicente Feola introduced the two young talents, and his team promptly marched off with the trophy.

If Garrincha was the second string to Pelé's lead in 1958, he moved to the first chair four years later. With his more famous teammate out injured, Garrincha took over the tournament. He was especially outstanding in the quarter- and semi-finals, which he completely dominated. He scored two and created the other against England, and notched another brace against Chile. The semi-final was a physical affair, and Garrincha finally lost his temper and was sent off. It took some smart manoeuvring behind the scenes to allow the winger to play in the Final. Once on the pitch he was relatively quiet, but Brazil still lifted the trophy.

Garrincha played most of his club football in Brazil, where he shone for a number of clubs, notably Botafogo and Corinthians. But it was on the international stage where Garrincha made his name, winning 50 caps for Brazil.

Brilliant dribbling skills and a super curling shot were Garrincha's main weapons, and he continued to display them into the mid-1960s. In 1965, however, he was involved in a car accident and was never quite the same again.

He was unfit when he made his World Cup farewell in 1966, although he did manage a scorching goal from a free kick against Bulgaria - a fitting goodbye from the greatest, and last, of his kind.

130

Juan Schiaffino

There were many great forwards on display in the 1950s, but few surpassed the skills or achievements of Juan Schiaffino. First for Uruguay, and later for AC Milan, Schiaffino shone brightly from his inside-forward position, where he combined great generalship with a sharp nose for a goal.

Having made his international debut at the age of 20 in 1945, Schiaffino continued to refine his skills, and was in full bloom by the time the World Cup re-opened its doors in 1950. After scoring twice against Bolivia, Schiaffino played a supporting role against Spain and Sweden. In the final match, Uruguay defeated hot favourites Brazil, with Schiaffino again on the score sheet.

If 1950 marked the high point of Schiaffino's career in terms of achievements, his own abilities probably reached their peak four years later in Switzerland. A goal against Czechoslovakia got him started, before he unleashed his full repertoire of skills against Scotland. Uruguay ran out 7-0 winners and moved on to face a famous England side. Another hammering ensued, with Schiaffino scoring the third of four Uruguayan goals.

The semi-final should have featured Puskas vs Schiaffino, the two greatest inside-lefts in world football. But Puskas was unfit and Schiaffino, who was also carrying an injury, was played out of position at centre-forward.

The third-place play-off defeat by Austria marked the end of Schiaffino's international career for Uruguay. He was transferred to Italy for a record £72,000, and immediately helped advance AC Milan to the top of the domestic game. In 1958, Schiaffino and Milan came as close as anyone had to deposing Real Madrid as European Champions. The Uruguayan scored a fine individual goal as Real came from a goal down to win in extra-time. Schiaffino made four appearances for Italy and wound down his career with two years at Roma.

Despite his slender build, Schiaffino had a complete game and rates as the finest forward ever produced by Uruguay.

BRAZIL: *Gilmar; Carlos Alberto, Júlio César, Djalma Santos, Nílton Santos; Dunga, Didi (Zico 78); Garrincha, Ademir (Romario 74), Pelé, Rivelino (Zagallo 81)*
Subs not used: *Claudio Taffarel, Edinho*
Goals: *Ademir 24, Pelé 26, 52*

URUGUAY: *Ladislao Mazurkiewicz; Victor Rodríguez Andrade, José Santamaría (William Martinez 56), José Nasazzi, Obdulio Varela, Shubert Gambetta; José Leandro Andrade, Hector Scarone (Pedro Rocha 64); Alcide Ghiggia (Luis Cubilla 80), Fernando Morena, Juan Schiaffino*
Subs not used: *Andrés Mazali, Oscar Omar Míguez*
Goal: *Morena 74*

Head-to-Head

Brazil	Vs	Uruguay	Edge
Gilmar		Mazurkiewicz	Uruguay
Carlso Alberto		Andrade Rodriguez	Brazil
Júlio César		José Nasazzi	Uruguay
Djalma Santos		José Santamaría	Even
Nílton Santos		Shubert Gambetta	Brazil
Dunga		Andrade	Uruguay
Didi		Varela	Even
Garrincha		Ghiggia	Brazil
Pele		Schiaffino	Brazil
Ademir		Morena	Brazil
Rivelino		Scarone	Even

Points: Brazil 6.5 Uruguay 4.5

WORLD CUP DECIDING MATCH, BRAZIL 1950

URUGUAY 2 BRAZIL 1

Uruguay were past masters in the World Cup, but it didn't matter. Brazil were huge favourites - playing at home and boasting the finest forwards in the world.

Uruguay had played only one first round match, an 8-0 whitewash of Bolivia, while Brazil had crushed Mexico, drawn with Switzerland and disposed of a decent Yugoslav side. In the Final Group, which replaced the semi-finals and Final, Brazil turned up the heat. Sweden fell 7-0 and Spain 6-1. Uruguay, by contrast, struggled to a 3-2 win over Sweden and were held to a draw by Spain. The final match left Uruguay needing a win, and

after the previous matches there seemed little prospect of that.

The first half was all Brazil. Cheered on by the frantic crowd of over 200,000, the famous inside forward trio of Zizinho, Ademir and Jair showed their unmatched skills. But Uruguay had made tactical adjustments to the old fashioned "Metodo" system. The two wing-halves were detailed to look after the Brazilian wingers on a full time basis, while the two full-backs, who operated as central defenders, were assisted by Varela, the attacking centre-half.

The modifications seemed to pay dividends in the first half because, despite a multitude of attacks and shots on goal, the game remained scoreless.

Brazil finally broke through almost immediately after half time. Ademir switched play from right to left to allow Friaça to put in a shot that Maspoli might have saved but didn't.

With Brazil 1-0 up and needing only a draw, pandamonia ensued. That's when Varela famously delayed the game. The great man also abandoned his defensive duties to resume a more attacking role. His pass out to the right saw little Ghiggia fly by Bigode and cross for Schiaffino, who volleyed home with his right foot.

Ghiggia was to be the key actor in the game's conclusion, but for now Brazil resumed the attack. Máspoli rose to the task and continued to keep Ademir and friends at bay.

Brazil's "diagonal" formation had also been somewhat modified as the tournament had progressed, but the left side of the defence remained relatively weak. If Bigode, the left-half who also had midfield duties, was beaten, there was little cover. That wasn't a good plan against Ghiggia, one of the tournaments premier players.

After 79 minutes, Ghiggia and Perez exchanged passes in a give and go, which saw the winger evade Bigode once again and head for goal. Schiaffino raced into the middle expecting another pass but Ghiggia spotted that Barbosa had left a gap at the near post and scored with a spinning shot.

The defeat left the crowd - and all of Brazil - in a state shock and depression. Beforehand, even many Uruguayans had feared the worst. Varela, who played a key role in making his team believe they could win, was philosophical in the years after the game:

"We won because we won, nothing more...If we had played one hundred times we would have won only that one."

ITALY 3 ARGENTINA 2

Both sides had looked impressive so far, in their own distinctly separate styles. Only Brazil and Holland had scored more goals than Argentina. No one had conceded as few as Italy. It seemed that the game would rest on whether Italy's vaunted man-markers could handle Maradona and Di Stefano, who at times had looked like something more than merely men.

Batistuta and Kempes would need to be kept in check too, and Maldini was moved to the middle to give his old pal Baresi a hand.

From the start Argentina attacked. Di Stefano took the reigns as usual, seemingly undeterred by Benetti's menacing presence. But each time Di Stefano broke free he found that his team mates were well covered. Bergomi and Maldini took a tight grip on Kempes and Baitstuta, and Tardelli paid special attention to Maradona. Even Burruchaga on the right was out of luck as he came face to face with Facchetti.

It was evident that Argentina's defenders would have to supplement the attack. Menotti had started Zanetti on the right specifically for that purpose, and it was he who provided the opener. Monti started the move, spraying a long ball towards Burruchaga who touched it past Facchetti. Zanetti reached it before his full-back rival and fired in a low skidding cross. Di Stefano hit it first time, and the vocal Argentine supporters went wild.

Italy's safe had been broken and it was time for some offensive thinking.

Giuseppe Meazza

Of all the fine playmaking inside-forwards in the 1930s, Giuseppe Meazza stood out and was arguably the decade's best player.

Meazza was one of only two players (fellow inside-forward Giovanni Ferrari was the other) to win the World Cup with Italy in both 1934 and 1938. A prolific goal scorer, Meazza was one of the first inside-forwards to also direct the play.

Meazza made his debut for Ambrosiana-Inter (now Inter Milan) in 1927 and led the league in scoring with 33 goals in 1928-1929. In 1930 he scored twice on his international debut against Switzerland. He continued to score goals for Italy for the next nine years. In all he made 53 appearances for his country and was on the score sheet 33 times, which remained a record not broken until the emergence of Luigi Riva. Two of those goals came in a rare defeat for Italy at the hands of England in 1934.

Surprisingly, Meazza scored only two goals in World Cup matches, but he created plenty, especially for Silvio Piola, his centre-forward partner in 1938.

At club level, Meazza and Piola were great rivals - the main goal scorers for the two best teams in the land. Piola's Juventus had the best of it; Inter only won two championships during Meazza's stay.

As well as being a magnificent player, Meazza was also a fine leader and was captain when Italy retained the World Cup on home soil. That victory was achieved despite intense pressure; Mussolini was watching and expected nothing less than victory.

Unlike many of the pre-war stars, Meazza is well remembered, his name immortalised as the official title of the San Siro stadium in Milan, an honour well deserved.

Meazza led the way, carefully evading his former team mate Monti and challenging Fillol with a dipping shot. Italy's full-backs could attack too, and Facchetti - who virtually invented the concept in the 1960s - surged forward. A sharp ball inside was turned on by Rivera, who immediately played in Rossi. Another Fillol save preserved Argentina's lead, but it didn't last long.

After Baresi played the ball out of defence, Piola did well to hold off Passarella and release Tardelli, who slightly miss-hit his shot but still found the back of the net.

Italy were in control and began to take advantage of Piola's dominance in the air. Argentina's defence was sturdy enough, but if it had a weakness it was

Diego Maradona

Commonly recognised as one of the three best players of all-time, Maradona might have ascended to the very top had it not been for his off-the-field shenanigans and less than sportsmanlike behaviour on the pitch. Pelé might be a better man, but was he really a better player?

It's safe to say that no one - Pelé included - has ever dominated a World Cup like Maradona did in 1986, and it's arguable that Maradona's displays in Mexico represent the best football ever played.

He provided a taster of what was to come in the group matches, creating all three against South Korea, scoring the equaliser in a 1-1 draw with Italy, and setting up the second as Bulgaria were defeated 2-0. He had a goal disallowed in the second round, and then in the quarter-final played his most famous match. Tensions between Argentina and England still remained after the Falklands Conflict, and Maradona took his own personal revenge. The infamous "Hand of God" goal revealed Maradona's dark side, while his second was the perfect demonstration of his rare talent. Starting in his own half he flew by Beardsley and Reid, who followed behind him like a lost dog. Maradona moved onwards, past Butcher and deceived Shilton with his finish. It was simply one the most breathtaking goals of all-time and deserves its recognition despite his earlier misdemeanour. Barry Davies was spot on: "You have to say that's magnificent. That was just pure fototball genius."

Maradona wasn't finished and repeated his one-man path of devastation in the semi-final. Belgium were swept aside with two more fine goals, the second of which featured another run in which he beat three opponents.

Lothar Matthäus subdued the little man in the Final, although Maradona still managed to steer a pass into the path of Jorge Burruchaga, who scored the winner. In seven matches Maradona had displayed all the qualities of a great attacking player; speed, strength, aggression, radar passing and sound finishing. There was nothing missing, except for a right foot - but even that hardly seemed to matter. Stanley Matthews, among others called him "the best one-footed player since Puskas". High praise, but possibly not high enough.

Mexico was the second of four World Cups in which Maradona featured, and in different ways he was a significant factor in each of them. Maradona nearly made it to a fifth, having been omitted from the 1978 squad at the very last minute.

In 1982 he was up and down. Quiet versus Belgium, unstoppable against Hungary and then subdued again. Claudio Gentile battered him into submission when Italy defeated Argentina in the second round, and in the next match against beautiful Brazil he finally snapped and was sent off for exacting revenge after some brutal treatment.

In 1984 Maradona began a seven-year spell with Napoli in Italy. He dragged the lowly side to two league titles and a Uefa Cup, but the pressure inside the Italian gold fish bowl was beginning to mount and Maradona's self discipline began to fade.

In the World Cup held in Italy in 1990, Argentina made it all the way to a showdown with West Germany as they attempted to retain their trophy. But the path to the Final wasn't the glorious trail it had been four years earlier.

Argentina were a team in decline and turned to rough-house tactics in order to survive. After losing to Cameroon, they barely scraped through to round two. In subsequent rounds they were regularly outplayed and twice advanced by way of penalties. Maradona was carrying an injury and was relatively quiet. He was once again closely marked and actually set a record for the number of times he was fouled. Several of the free kicks were awarded, however, after some outrageous Maradona dives.

Before the semi-final with Italy, which was staged in Naples, Maradona pleaded with the fans to support him rather than the home team. The Italian fans turned on him but it was Argentina that advanced after another penalty shoot-out. The luck finally ran out against West Germany, and Maradona turned on the tears, but there was little sympathy from the Italians.

In 1991, Maradona failed a drug test and was banned from the game for 15 months. Napoli lost the battle to keep him when he was reinstated, and he briefly played in Spain before returning to Argentina.

It seemed we'd heard the last from Maradona, but as the 1994 World Cup approached, Argentina were struggling. After a great deal of fuss, Maradona was restored to the team, and immediately turned things around. In the early matches in the USA he looked almost his old self. Passing the ball as well as ever and scoring a fine goal against Greece. Argentina were suddenly contenders, and then Maradona's world fell apart once again. He failed a drug test and was ejected from the tournament and banned from football. The rollercoaster was finally over. The ride with Maradona was thrilling and sickening all at once.

dealing with aerial assaults. Ruggeri was stretched to his limit and a mistake seemed just a matter of time. After 72 minutes, Piola met Maldini's angled ball with tremendous power to head past Fillol.

Time was running short for Argentina, who desperately needed to find some space. Di Stefano moved forward while Kempes dropped back and took over the playmaking. The switch did the trick as Italy's defence was momentarily pulled out of position. Maradona took advantage, slipping between Bergomi and Baresi and lifting his shot over Zoff. The little man had been virtually dormant, but one lapse had let him in and Argentina were back on level terms.

Argentina had the momentum as they began extra time. The Italians had been three minutes away from the semi-finals, but instead faced another half an hour trying to hold off Di Stefano and his posse.

Kempes, sensing another chance to steal the show in extra-time, surged through the middle to provide Orsi with a chance, but Zoff and Italy held on.

Suddenly, Italy struck the knock-out blow. Meazza received a clearance from Maldini and turned it on towards Luigi Riva, a former winger who'd come on to add pace to the attack. Italy's champion goal scorer sped by Monti and slowed slightly before accelerating past Passarella and scoring with a fabulous shot high to Fillol's right.

After 106 minutes - and without warning - it was all over. Italy's defence had held on for long enough to allow their forwards to show their hand. Di Stefano stood in the centre circle in disbelief, no doubt cursing the golden goal rule. It was tough on the great man, and on Maradona too - the tournament would be the poorer for their loss. But all credit to Italy, who'd kept their composure in the face of superior skills. Perhaps they knew their history; until Brazil in 1958 the most skilful team never to have won the World Cup.

ITALY: *Dino Zoff; Marco Tardelli, Giuseppe Bergomi, Franco Baresi, Paolo Maldini, Giacinto Facchetti; Romeo Benetti, Gianni Rivera, (Sandro Mazzola 82), Giuseppe Meazza; Silvio Piola (Luigi Riva 90), Roberto Baggio (Paolo Rossi 68)*
Subs not used: *Giampiero Combi, Riccardo Ferri*
Goals: *Tardelli 36, Piola 72, Riva 106*

ARGENTINA: *Ubaldo Fillol; Javier Zanetti, Daniel Passarella, Oscar Ruggeri, Silvio Marzolini; Luis Monti; Jorge Burruchaga (Antonio Rattin 90), Alfredo Di Stefano, Diego Maradona; Mario Kempes, Gabriel Batistuta (Raimundo Orsi 84)*
Subs not used: *Amedeo Carrizo, Jorge Olguin, Juan Manuel Moreno*
Goals: *Di Stefano 27, Maradona 87*

Head-to-Head

Italy	Vs	Argentina	Edge
Zoff		Fillol	Italy
Bergomi		Zanetti	Even
Baresi		Passarella	Even
Maldini		Ruggeri	Italy
Facchetti		Marzolini	Even
Benetti		Monti	Argentina
Tardelli		Burruchaga	Italy
Meazza		Di Stefano	Argentina
Rivera		Maradona	Argentina
Baggio		Kempes	Even
Piola		Batistuta	Italy

Italy 6.5 Argentina 4.5

GERMANY 2 ENGLAND 1

Helmut Schön was still seeking his best line-up and this time tried Overath on the left with Beckenbauer returning to the defence.

Ramsey was still searching for the answers at centre-back and asked Duncan Edwards to deal with the great Gerd Müller. After an encouraging performance against Sweden, Beckham was called to partner Robson in the middle, with Finney restored on the left.

England certainly started with confidence. Although in recent years the Germans have dominated their great rivals (nine wins, three draws and four defeats for Germany or West Germany since 1970), for many years the boot was on the other foot. England didn't lose to the Germans until 1968, and several of the England side had fond memories of this fixture.

Stanley Matthews, for example, was on the winning side each of the four times he met Germany. In this game he imposed himself immediately. Without a left-winger, Schön would depend on Andreas Brehme to provide width, but he had to deal with Matthews first. The English knight won the initial encounter, accelerating to the by-line and crossing to the near post. Lineker was there first but couldn't hit the target.

England's top striker soon atoned for his profligacy. Edwards advanced from defence and started a neat move, providing a square ball for Charlton who

139

Bobby Moore

Bobby Moore wasn't the typical British central defender. The headed clearance and long hoof upfield were alien concepts to England's greatest defender. A tremendous understanding of the game and remarkable leadership abilities made Moore one of the most respected footballers of his era. Although lacking in pace, and not the best in the air, Moore's ability to see danger before it became troublesome, allied with a ferocious tackle and tidy use of the ball, helped him stay at the top of the world game for over a decade.

Moore was Player of the Tournament when he captained England to the World Cup in 1966. In the final minute of the game it was Moore's cool control of the ball and visionary pass that sent Hurst away for his famous third goal - the perfect demonstration of Moore's composure under pressure. For the next four years, England were probably the best side in the world. They should never have lost in the semi-finals of the European Championship in 1968, and it wasn't until the World Cup defence that they were truly surpassed as the world's best. In Mexico, Moore played possibly his most famous game, duelling with Pelé, who called him: "...my friend, the finest and most honourable defender I ever played against."

The defeat in the quarter-finals by West Germany marked the beginning of the end for Moore. He was still a key figure when Netzer took England to the cleaners in the European Championships in 1972, but his powers were on the wane, and a year later, his international career was over. He won 107 caps in total, although when he retired the tally was actually 108, as until 2001 matches against FIFA were recognised as full internationals.

His international odyssey began in 1962 when he displaced Bobby Robson from the England team in time to take part in his first World Cup finals. Back then Moore's "un-English" style of play raised questions with the critics and it wasn't until he lifted the Jules Rimet that the doubts really subsided.

Moore played most of his career with West Ham United, with whom he won the FA Cup in 1964, and the European Cup-Winners Cup the following season. He ended his career with Fulham in 1976 and then took up various managerial and executive posts with limited success.

In 1993 Moore died of cancer at the age of 51. Gone, but forever remembered as the one of the game's finest ambassadors and greatest defenders.

weaved inside Kohler before feeding Lineker. Maier came out to meet him but couldn't stop the crisp shot.

The Germans were down but had experience of comebacks against England. Indeed, five of the starting line-up helped West Germany recover from two goals down in the 1970 World Cup quarter-final. Gordon Banks didn't play in that game, cast down by illness, and he showed what his team had missed with a string of fine saves. First, Rahn banged a cross-shot towards the far post and Banks tipped over. From the corner, Kohler nodded against the bar and Banks grabbed Müller's stabbed effort at the rebound.

It was evident that the midfield battle would be crucial. Matthäus worked overtime to quell Robson and Beckham, and although Schuster wasn't one for a fight, he certainly knew how to create space. It was he who laid on the equaliser, evading Robson and moving past Edwards before playing in Müller. Banks had no answer.

Both sides had chances to take the lead before half-time; Robson volleyed over Charlton's centre before Beckenbauer carved his way through England's defence and hit the post. The best chance of all came via a trademark Beckham free kick, but the athletic Maier saved well.

Ramsey brought on Gascoigne at the break, hoping he'd have more influence than Finney. But the winger's departure allowed Berti Vogts to attach himself to Charlton, and England's most effective playmaker was not the same threat in the second half. Schuster was quiet too, but Germany had more creative options. Beckenbauer came into the midfield and started to dictate the rhythm. Moore was forced to make a timely intervention when Rummenigge turned on a ball from his captain, and only Banks could have saved Müller's close-range effort.

If England had hope, it lay with the Matthews-Lineker connection. As the final seconds ticked down, Brehme was again defeated on the right and Matthews provided another curling cross. It fell sweetly onto Lineker's right foot only for Maier to miraculously save. Even Banks had to applaud.

Extra time was needed, which historically favoured Germany. In four games between the two countries that required an additional 30 minutes, only the 1966 Final was decided in England's favour.

The "Golden Goal" rule was in effect and the game was on a knife-edge. Ramsey sent on Michael Owen for Charlton in the hope that his youthful zest and sense for the big occasion would tilt the balance. The move almost paid off as Owen got the first chance to settle it. Beckham's through ball saw the little striker race through and chip over Maier, who looked back in relief as the ball trickled wide.

Just as English minds began to wander to a penalty shoot-out, Müller struck a cruel blow. Overath's ball looked innocent enough, with Edwards and Moore both to hand. But the German striker stole through the middle and thumped a half-volley past Banks.

After another cliffhanger, England had again fallen over the edge. They'd acquitted themselves well, but the better team had won. Moore, Edwards, Lineker and even Beckham looked as good as their legends suggested - but Beckenbauer, Matthäus and Müller were a step ahead.

Gerd Müller

Arguably the greatest goal scorer in the history of international football, Gerd Müller scored a mind-boggling 68 times in 62 internationals. Only three players; Puskas, Pelé and Kocsis, have scored more international goals than "Der Bomber", but all played in times when goals came more easily. In the modern era, no player has come close to Müller's goals-to-games ratio - or showed such a knack for scoring on the big occasion.

Between 1970 and 1975, Müller scored two goals in a World Cup semi-final, two goals in a European Championship Final, the winning goal in a World Cup Final and three goals in two European Cup Final appearances. No one, not Van Basten or Di Stefano, not Puskas or Klinsmann, not even Pelé can match that record, nor Müller's total of 14 goals in 13 World Cup finals matches.

Müller's road to greatness was not always a smooth one. When he arrived at Bayern Munich in 1964, his coach dismissed him as too small: "I'm not putting that little elephant in among my string of thoroughbreds" is the famous quote from Tschik Cajkovski. But soon the stocky striker was a first team regular as Bayern began their assent towards the top of the European game. Bayern won three European Cups between 1974 and 1976, the first two inspired by Müller.

West Germany were also on the rise. After 10 Müller goals had helped the Germans to the semis in the 1970 World Cup, they marched to an easy triumph in the 1972 European Championships and, despite an ageing team, held on to defeat Cruyff's Holland in 1974 courtesy of a typical piece of Müller finishing.

Often dismissed by naysayers as "merely a goal scorer", Müller was in fact a fine all-round footballer who despite his short stature also scored many with his head. By the end, after a career including 365 goals in the German league, there were few critics left.

GERMANY: *Sepp Maier; Berti Vogts, Jürgen Kohler, Franz Beckenbauer, Andreas Brehme (Karl-Heinz Schnellinger 104); Helmut Rahn, Lothar Matthäus, Bernd Schuster (Fritz Walter 73), Wolfgang Overath; Karl-Heinz Rummenigge (Jürgen Klinsmann 87), Gerd Müller*
Subs not used: *Jürgen Croy, Günther Netzer*
Goals: *Müller 31, 112*

ENGLAND: *Gordon Banks; Jimmy Armfield, Bobby Moore, Duncan Edwards, Ray Wilson; Stanley Matthews, Bryan Robson, David Beckham, Tom Finney (Paul Gascoigne 45); Bobby Charlton (Michael Owen 98); Gary Lineker*
Subs not used: *Peter Shilton, Tony Adams*
Goal: *Lineker 24*

Head-to-Head

Germany	Vs	England	Edge
Maier		Banks	England
Vogts		Armfield	Germany
Beckenbauer		Moore	Germany
Kohler		Edwards	England
Brehme		Wilson	Germany
Rahn		Matthews	England
Matthäus		Robson	Germany
Schuster		Beckham	Even
Overath		Charlton	England
Rummenigge		Finney	Germany
Müller		Lineker	Germany

Points: Germany 6.5 England 4.5

WORLD CUP QUARTER-FINAL, MEXICO 1970

WEST GERMANY 3 ENGLAND 2

England and Germany, arch-rivals on and off the pitch, have played some dramatic matches over the years. Those two semi-finals in 1990 and 1996 stand out for drama value, and 1966 had a mystique all of its own, but it's the World Cup quarter-final of 1970 that stands as arguably the most important. Why? Because before the game, and 81 minutes into this one, England were World Champions, possibly the best team in the world, and seemingly on their way to another World Cup Final. Moreover, they were absolutely unafraid of the Germans who had beaten them only once in forty years of trying. A little over half an hour later, West Germany had won and would keep on winning, against England and against everyone else.

England advanced to the quarter-finals as runners-up in Group Three, having lost to Brazil in a thriller and beaten Romania and Czechoslovakia. West Germany won their group, but wins over Bulgaria, Peru and Morocco weren't enough to frighten England, who were slight favourites.

The odds on West Germany shortened slightly when England goalkeeper Gordon Banks went down with food poisoning, but for over an hour it didn't seem to matter. After an untidy opening spell of few genuine openings, and in which wild tackles flowed freely, England made the breakthrough. Alan Mullery, a typical 1970s chopper, except for the fact that he could actually play football, both created and finished it. After supplying a long diagonal ball to Newton on the right he charged forward and connected with a half-volley from 10 yards.

The match settled again and it wasn't until five minutes after half-time that England scored again. Newton was again the provider with a second excellent cross. Peters arrived late to force it home. England were 2-0 up and looked home and dry.

Within seven minutes, West German coach Helmut Schön had taken action. Grabowski came on for Libuda and helped turn the match with a signature run that supplied Löhr with a good chance. England's Charlton almost made it three with a typical swerving run matched with an uncharacteristically weak shot.

It was Beckenbauer who brought the Germans back into it, exchanging passes with Fichtel before letting fly from the edge of the area. Bonetti might have saved it - Banks almost certainly would have - but as it slipped beneath the keeper the deficit was cut to one.

Alf Ramsey brought on Colin Bell for Bobby Charlton, a move that is often said to have cost England the game. Several of the England players later said they were surprised by the move and that it gave the Germans a psychological edge, but it made sense at the time. Besides, Bell soon supplied a cross from which Hurst missed the target by a matter of inches. Had the big man scored, Ramsey's move would have been heralded as genius.

With less than ten minutes left on the clock, Seeler got the back of his head to Schnellinger's cross and Bonetti was beaten again.

Beckenbauer nearly scored at the end but as so often in matches between these two rivals, extra-time was required. Although the momentum belonged to the Germans, it was England who created the better chances. But after Hurst nodded over, Grabowski made his mark, skinning the tiring Cooper and crossing for Löhr who played it back in. Müller volleyed home in his own definitive style.

Still England pressed forward and were unlucky not to get a penalty when Beckenbauer appeared to pull down Bell (him again!). Newton and Müllery came close in the dying seconds, but it wasn't to be.

West Germany were through and the tide had gone out on England's brief spell at the top of the football world. Many thought that the better side had lost, and certainly England had their chances, but look at the names on the German team sheet. Beckenbauer, Seeler, Overath in midfield; Müller and Grabowski up front; Schulz, Schnellinger, Vogts and Maier at the back - all of them great players. England had their stars too, but the side's best player was on his way out. Bobby Charlton had played his last international. England have never been the same since.

HOLLAND 2 FRANCE 1

There were similarities between these two sides and their football histories. Both countries struggled in the first half of the century, only to blossom in recent years. Both Holland and France have produced two stellar teams in the last 30 years - Holland in the early 1970s and late 80s, and France in the mid 1980s and late 1990s. Each country boasted a host of individual stars, including a total of seven European Footballers of the Year (although Papin was only on the French bench). Both countries have a tradition of fluid, flowing football, but at times both France - and especially Holland - have been found wanting when it mattered most.

Michel Platini

The greatest French player of all-time, Michel Platini might have challenged the legends of Cruyff and even Pelé had France lifted the World Cup under his leadership.

As it was, France lost twice in the semi-finals, which left the 1984 European Championship as the crowning achievement of Platini's fabulous career. Although most famous for his vision and passing, Platini also possessed a sharp cutting edge. He scored 41 international goals in 72 internationals, including five in three appearances in the World Cup finals.

There are those who believe that Platini under-achieved in World Cups, but then the bar was always set at a great altitude. Certainly in 1978 - when Platini was an emerging star - France disappointed, failing to progress past round one. But in 1982, Platini played his part as France progressed to the semis, only to lose on penalties to West Germany. Four years later, and now a veteran of 31, Platini drifted in and out of the tournament, mixing anonymity with brilliance. He scored the equaliser in the quarter-final with Brazil but then shot over the bar in the penalty shoot-out. France again fell to West Germany, an infinitely less skilful team, but then Platini wasn't fully fit.

When in top form - especially in those European Championships - he was the most dominant footballer on the planet, and the most beautiful to watch too. He scored nine goals in five finals games, helping to make light of his team's lack of a great striker, which is perhaps the real reason for the World Cup disappointments.

Platini won the first of three successive European Footballer of the Year awards in 1983 while starring for Juventus. The Italian club won two league titles, a European Cup Winners Cup and, amid tragedy at Heysel, the European Cup in 1985 under Platini's guidance. Despite the claims of Monti, Charles and Zidane, Platini is rated by Juventus fans as their club's greatest player, an honour in itself.

Platini started his career with AS Nancy-Lorraine, where he won a French Cup before moving on to AS Saint-Etienne, with whom he won the French league prior to departing for Italy.

Platini retired in 1987 and briefly managed the national team with limited success. But Platini's full impact on French football wasn't felt until 1998 when a generation of players inspired by Michel Platini finally lifted the World Cup.

THE MATCHES

With so much skill on display, a football feast should have been on the menu, but it didn't start that way as the two defences took the upper hand. Desailly and Rijkaard, stars for AC Milan in midfield, were just as good for their countries in the centre of defence. Here they faced tough opponents, Van Basten and Fontaine; two excellent strikers cut down by injuries in their primes. Desailly's task was probably the tougher. Van Basten is arguably the most complete of all strikers, although interestingly Fontaine scored more international goals in less than half the number of caps.

With the main goal threats under special watch, the onus was on the attacking midfielders to break the deadlock.

Cruyff looked the best on show - even in comparison with Platini, Zidane and Kopa. Fleet of foot and mind, he crafted the first opening after half an hour. Working behind Van Basten, he deceived Thuram and drifted past Deschamps. His through-ball found Gullit, but Bossis was there and forced a corner.

Platini took up the challenge, lofting a long laser-guided pass through to Kopa, but the shot was hit straight at Van Beveren. Neeskens was again a force, but in Zidane he found a new breed of playmaker. Gone are the days of the skilled waif. Today's midfield general can handle himself in the trenches as well as command his troops. Zidane's strength created the best chance of the half. Fending off former Juventus team mate Davids, he went past Koeman, and after a quick foot shuffle, beat the keeper only to find the upright.

Within ten minutes of the restart after half-time, the game was virtually dead. Cruyff was brought down by Jonquet just outside the area. To Koeman, free kicks from that range represented a virtual penalty and, true to form, a curling rocket left Barthez stranded.

Cruyff scored the second himself, slotting home comfortably after a neat exchange of passes with Gullit. There was still time for France to come back, but they didn't seem to believe it. This should have been Platini's time, but he couldn't rid himself of Davids. Zidane's luck was no better, and shorn of their two great creators, France ran out of ideas.

Rijkaard and Gullit both had chances to score a third as the Dutch began to emphasise the gulf between the two teams. On paper they looked well matched; each side fielding a talented defence, a couple of playmakers, and a deadly goal scorer. But in every instance, Holland's version was a little superior.

At least Fontaine won his bout with Rijkaard, as he knocked in a consolation goal as time ran out, but it was Rijkaard and Holland who were left standing at the end.

147

HOLLAND: *Jan van Beveren; Wim Suurbier, Ronald Koeman, Frank Rijkaard, Ruud Krol; Edgar Davids, Johan Neeskens, Wim van Hanegem (Dennis Bergkamp 66); Ruud Gullit, Marco van Basten (Rob Rensenbrink 76), Johan Cruyff*
Subs not used: *Edwin van der Sar, Frank de Boer, Marc Overmars*
Goals: *Koeman 49, Cruyff 54*

FRANCE: *Fabian Barthez; Lilian Thuram, Marcel Desailly, Robert Jonquet (Manuel Amaros 75), Maxime Bossis; Jean Tigana (Alain Giresse 65);, Didier Deschamps; Raymond Kopa (Roger Piantoni 82), Michel Platini, Zinedine Zidane; Just Fontaine*
Suns not used: *Joel Bats, Jenn-Pierre Papin*
Goal: *Fontaine 85*

Head-to-Head

Holland	Vs	France	Edge
Van Beveren		Barthez	Holland
Suurbuer		Thuram	France
Koeman		Jonquet	Holland
Rijkaard		Desailly	France
Krol		Bossis	Holland
Neeskens		Deschamps	Holland
Davids		Tigana	France
Van Hanegem		Zidane	France
Gullit		Kopa	Holland
Van Basten		Fontaine	Holland
Cruyff		Platini	Holland

Points: Holland 7 France 4

Marco van Basten

But for the injuries that prematurely ended his career, Marco van Basten might have challenged Gerd Müller as Europe's greatest-ever striker. Even in his relatively short career, Van Basten rose to heights that few others have ever reached.

Like so many Dutch stars, Van Basten started his career with Ajax. He won the Golden Boot as Europe's top scorer in 1986 when scoring 37 goals, attracting the attention of AC Milan.

With Ruud Gullit and Frank Rijkaard, Van Basten formed a devastating Dutch trio that propelled Milan to the pinnacle of European football. With the Italian club he won three league titles and two European Cups. In the first of those European triumphs in 1989, Van Basten and Gullit put on one of the great performances, hammering Steaua Bucharest with two goals apiece. That performance helped Van Basten to the second of three European Footballer of the Year awards. He was also the second FIFA World Footballer of the Year.

Tall and strong, but with all the skills as well, Van Basten was a devastating goal scorer with every team he represented, including Holland's national team. After failing to qualify for the World Cup in 1986, Holland finally put it together and lifted the European title two years later. Van Basten was in magnificent form in Germany, scoring a hat trick against England, the winner in the semi against West Germany and a tremendous volley to seal Holland's triumph in the Final. Holland didn't fair so well in the World Cup in Italy with Van Basten strangely out of sorts - but he was soon back on form for Milan.

In all, Van Basten notched 24 goals in 58 games for Holland, and 128 in 143 for Ajax. Even at Milan - against the greatest defenders in the world - he kept up his scoring rate with 90 in 147 games.

Sadly, after struggling with injury all season, Van Basten was unable to inspire Milan in another European Cup Final in 1993 - his last competitive match. For the millions of football fans in awe of Van Basten's skills it all ended far too early - but it was fun while it lasted.

Semi-finals

BRAZIL 3 ITALY 2

Each of the five meetings between Brazil and Italy in the World Cup has been of great importance. On four of those occasions, the winner of the match went on to lift the World Cup. On the fifth occasion, in 1978, Brazil beat Italy in the third-place playoff.

The form of these two teams in the earlier rounds suggested that the winner of this match might again go on to bigger things. As it is every time they clash the game hinges on a simple question: Would Brazil's superior attack find a way through Italy's stronger defence?

After Pelé's sensational performance against Uruguay, he received close attention from Bergomi - but then the Italians man-marked all the main dangers: Benetti on Didi, Maldini on Ademir, with Facchetti keeping tabs on Garrincha.

From the start Brazil stroked the ball around, patiently looking for the gaps. Dunga, one of the few Brazilians without a personal escort, took up much of the playmaking, but the chances were few and far between. After 25 minutes Carlos Alberto overlapped Garrincha and crossed to the near post. Ademir was there but Zoff beat him to it and coolly palmed away. Pelé found room to play Rivelino in on the half hour mark but the covering Baresi made a decisive tackle and cleared the danger. That was about it in the first half. Plenty of probing and searching, but precious few shots on goal. Italy had just one attempt; Rivera skipped away from Zito and sent Baggio through the middle. As Gilmar closed him down, Baggio over-ran and put his shot into the side-netting.

The second half started with a bang. Garrincha for once got the better of Facchetti on the right and moved in towards goal. As Baresi closed in, the Brazilian swerved away from goal and found room to chip back into the area. Pelé was on hand to sweep it past Zoff and give Brazil a deserved lead.

Brazil were in the mood and Didi decided he'd had enough of Benetti. A turn, a feint, another turn, and he was free, Rivelino was the beneficiary of the pass and fired a first time ball towards Pelé. The great man helped the ball on its way and Garrincha connected with a thumping shot which left Zoff dumbstruck.

If Italy needed a wake-up call, they'd just received it. Two goals down and with less than 25 minutes left to play, something special was called for. Riva came on for Piola, who'd been ineffectual against Djalma Santos, and Meazza

150

Paolo Maldini

He made his league debut at 16, played his first international at 19, and soon developed into the finest full-back in the world.

Maldini had a great footballing pedigree. His father, Cesare, was captain of both AC Milan and Italy from his position in the centre of defence. Later, Cesare would coach the Italian team captained by his son.

Paolo Maldini succeeded Antonio Cabrini in the Italian team in 1988 and hasn't looked back since. The world got a first good look at the young left-back at the European Championships, but it was for his club AC Milan that he first showed his true worth.

Together with Italian teammate Franco Baresi, and the Dutch trio of Gullit, Van Basten and Rijkaard, Maldini helped Milan supplant Liverpool as Europe's dominant team. He played in all three of Milan's European Cup triumphs and by the early 1990s, he'd succeeded Baresi as the best defender in Europe.

In 1990, Italy were World Cup favourites mainly because their defence, in which Maldini was a key part, was practically impregnable. The defence did its bit, but Italy fell in the semi-finals. Maldini was back four years later and this time Italy made it to the Final. En route, Maldini had moved from left-back to centre-back in order to cover for the injured Baresi. He adapted with customary brilliance and many observers said that he was now the world's best in two positions. He remained at centre-back when Baresi returned for the Final, and Italy kept another clean sheet, but again lost in a penalty shoot-out.

It didn't get any better for Italy or Maldini in the World Cup. By 1998 he was captain and his side progressed serenely to the quarter-finals where they fell - in another penalty shoot-out - to the hosts France.

Italy's record in European Championships was unimpressive until 2000, when Italy again fell to France in a Final. Along the way they'd showed incredible resilience to hold off Holland with 10 men.

The defence - now including the impressive Nesta and Cannavaro - was probably the best in the tournament and gave reason to believe that in 2002, Italy and Maldini might finally lift the World Cup. It would be no more than the great defender deserves.

began to look for ways to set the speedster free. After Tardelli came inside to win the ball, Meazza paused for a moment and then flicked a dangerous ball between Brazil's central pillars. Riva was onto it and moved into range, but Nílton Santos stole the ball as Riva prepared to pull the trigger.

Brazil seemed to be headed for the Final and then, suddenly, Riva leapt in to intercept Dunga's pass and immediately released Rivera who let fly from 25 yards. It was a stunning goal - one of the best of the tournament - and it gave Italy renewed belief. Rivera and Meazza were in charge now, exchanging sharp passes and looking for runners. Maldini obliged, galloping through from the back. His long run was stopped when Alberto slid in and conceded the foul. Baggio floated it in and Gilmar fluffed the clearance. Tardelli pounced and lashed in another crucial goal. He didn't score too many, but when he did, they tended to matter.

Brazil were shocked - this was the Maracana all over again. Italy saw their chance and went for the jugular. Facchetti centred from the left and Riva connected with a sharp header that Gilmar tipped over. From Meazza's corner, Djalma Santos could only head out towards the left touchline. Nílton Santos retrieved it and, cool as ever, played a long diagonal ball to Garrincha. The winger ran straight through the middle and jinked past Bergomi. Baresi came to meet him, but Garrincha squeezed a pass to the open Ademir. Zoff was beaten again and Italy's sky came tumbling down.

Great offence had overcome great defence, but only by the narrowest of margins. For once, Italy had been consistently good throughout the tournament and would have made worthy finalists. But no neutral could be too upset. Magnificent as Baresi and Maldini were, you'd always prefer to watch Pelé or Garrincha, who with every match seemed to push back the boundaries of the game.

BRAZIL: *Gilmar; Carlos Alberto, Júlio César, Djalma Santos, Nílton Santos; Dunga, Didi (Gérson 74); Garrincha, Ademir (Romario 88), Pelé, Roberto Rivelino*
Subs not used: *Claudio Taffarel, Edinho, Mário Zagallo*
Goals: *Pelé 47, Garrincha 72, Ademir 90*

ITALY: *Dino Zoff; Marco Tardelli, Giuseppe Bergomi, Franco Baresi, Paolo Maldini, Giacinto Facchetti; Romeo Benetti, Gianni Rivera, Giuseppe Meazza; Silvio Piola (Luigi Riva 69), Roberto Baggio (Paolo Rossi 88)*
Subs not used: *Giampiero Combi, Riccardo Ferri, Sandro Mazzola*
Goals: *Rivera 79, Tardelli 85*

Head-to-Head

Brazil	Vs	Italy	Edge
Gilmar		Zoff	Italy
Carlos Alberto		Bergomi	Brazil
Nílton Santos		Facchetti	Even
Djalma Santos		Maldini	Italy
Júlio César		Baresi	Italy
Dunga		Benetti	Even
Garrincha		Tardelli	Brazil
Didi		Meazza	Brazil
Rivelino		Rivera	Even
Pelé		Baggio	Brazil
Ademir		Piola	Even

Points: Brazil 6 Italy 5

WORLD CUP SECOND ROUND, BARCELONA 1982

ITALY 3 BRAZIL 2

The ultimate demonstration of the irremovable finally bringing a halt to the irresistible.

Brazil were back at their very best. After 12 years of mediocre football, Zico, Falcao and Socrates revived the memories of 1970 and were poetry in motion in their early games. Ten goals in the first three matches hinted at their dominance, but you had to see Brazil play to truly appreciate their level. Beautiful passing movements, spectacular shooting; the boys in blue and gold had it all. They continued their demonstration in the second round group matches, reaching for the sky as they thrashed Argentina, who'd added Maradona to the winning side of 1978.

Italy by contrast were in turmoil. Poland, Peru and Cameroon all held the Azzuri, who qualified only on goal difference and had scored just twice in round one.

153

But Italy lifted their game to also beat Argentina and at least looked worthy opponents for Brazil, who only needed a draw to progress to the semi-finals. For once, Italy were forced to show their full hand and the result was a magnificent match - one of the best in any World Cup. Italy took an early lead when Cabrini advanced down the left and crossed after a nice ball from Conti. Rossi was on to it and headed firmly past Brazil's suspect keeper. No one knew it at the time, but Paolo was about to catch fire in this tournament and secure his World Cup legend.

Before he could do any further damage here though, Brazil struck back. Having conjured a chance that Serginho wasted, Zico turned beautifully and passed to Socrates, who evaded Scirea and shot powerfully past Zoff.

Brazil virtually gifted Rossi his second. Cerezo's loose pass was intercepted by the razor sharp Italian, who fired in from just inside the area.

In the second half, Rossi surprisingly missed a good chance, slicing his shot wide from close range. Brazil looked to punish the error. Junior, the marvellous attacking left-back, made a run down his wing and fed Falcao, whose terrific left-footed drive levelled the match and put Brazil in pole position.

Italy had played well to get to this position, and now they had to find another goal. Luckily, in Rossi they possessed the perfect weapon. His speed and skill were ideally suited to Italy's counter-attacking game. The winner came from a set-piece, however. Much is made of Brazil's disinterest in defence, but when the crucial goal was conceded they had plenty of troops in place. Conti's corner eventually came to Rossi who scored with ease.

Brazil looked for the equaliser, but Zoff - who was in an altogether different league than his opposite number - kept the golden tide at bay and Italy were through.

It was a shame that FIFA's strange two-group phase format produced this match in the second round rather than in the Final, but it counts as a classic nonetheless.

Brazil were a wonderful side, one of the fans' favourites, but Italy were more than a match, at least on the day.

The Italians went on to lift the World Cup, underlining the quality of their team, which, with Zoff, Scirea, Tardelli and Rossi, included as many great players as any team in the last twenty years.

THE MATCHES

GERMANY 2 HOLLAND 2
(Germany wins 5-4 on penalties)

Every time Holland produces a great team, Germany manages to find one to match it. First in 1974 and again in 1990, Holland were the World Cup favourites, only to find that West Germany had put together a stellar side of their own. As it was on both those occasions, Holland had looked the more skilful side in this tournament, while the Germans were as efficient as ever.

One man with a particular point to prove was Johan Cruyff. In 1974, he'd lost his personal duel with Berti Vogts, which proved a critical blow to his country's chances. Holland hoped for better from their captain in the rematch.

The Dutch started quickly, Neeskens stripping Walter and bursting forward. His long-range effort didn't trouble Maier, but a warning had been served. Cruyff was in defiant mood and began to give little Vogts the runaround. Turning his man on the half way line he headed in field and then cut back to feed Krol, who was charging down the left. Rahn, of course, didn't feel the compulsion to follow him, and the full-back looked to capitalise on the room. He exchanged passes with Van Hanegem before flashing a shot across the face of the goal. Maier couldn't reach it but Gullit could, and tapped home the opening goal.

The Germans had been in worse holes than this and refused to panic. When Cruyff and Krol again combined to create a wasted chance for Van Basten, Germany's great captains took charge. Matthäus moved to the right to help Vogts and - when needed - Beckenbauer stepped forward to fill the midfield void.

With Germany paying him extra attention, Cruyff began to fade. Holland turned to Van Hanegem to direct play and it was his pass after 33 minutes that released Gullit. Brehme was beaten on the inside and the dreadlocked star shot fiercely. Maier pulled off one of the saves of the tournament, rising to the occasion as he usually did.

The save proved critical. The Dutch began to wonder whether this was destined to be another German day. When Van Basten's shot bounced safely off the post just before half-time, the Germans began to believe they had a chance too.

Willy Schulz replaced Walter at the break, allowing Beckenbauer to take up permanent residence in midfield. The midfield line-ups now read like a Hall of Fame roll call; Matthäus, Beckenbauer and Overath versus Neeskens, Van Hanegem and Rijkaard. The Germans seemed to edge the battle and crept back into the game. When Beckenbauer dispossessed his great rival Cruyff, there seemed little danger. But a long pass gave Rummenigge room on the left. A quick charge past Suurbier was rounded off with a blast into the top left-hand corner. The German had been quiet so far in the tournament but emerged at just the right time.

Holland's confidence was draining fast, and with Cruyff under close surveillance it was up to Gullit to reinvigorate his side. Brehme was with him but Gullit carried on regardless. The German was almost on top of him as he progressed to the edge of the box, but the Dutchman still got his shot in and the unsighted Maier didn't move.

At last, Holland looked to be on their way. Rijkaard might have finished it when he fired over after a neat ball from Neeskens.

Germany, of course, continued to believe. The front pair finally got into the game with eleven minutes to go. Rummenigge nipped past Krol and gave Müller his first chance, but Van Beveren was equal to stabbed shot. A moment later Rummenigge repeated the move, this time beating Koeman. Müller knew what was coming and moved to the near post. Hulshoff desperately tried to reach him but was too late to stop the volley.

Extra time saw Holland attempt to reassert control, but Cruyff was struggling again and his main striker was having a tough time. Van Basten put one header over the bar but was otherwise stifled by the German defence. Poor Marco had received some top class attention during the tournament. Schesternev, Germano, Desailly, and now the impressive Kohler - it was a compliment of sorts, but not one Van Basten enjoyed.

A Matthäus shot came off the post in the dying seconds, and Klinsmann was oh so close to connecting with the rebound, but it wasn't to be.

After two hours, penalties were needed for the first time in the tournament. Germany, of course, had plenty of experience in that department, while Holland had experience, but not any they'd want to remember.

The first eight spot kicks were faultless, the work of some fine ball strikers. Overath, who possessed a mean left foot himself, stepped up, but Van Beveren saved. Dutch delight turned to sorrow when Bergkamp's shot rattled the crossbar. Brehme made no mistake to restore the German lead, which left the burden on the broad shoulders of Van Hanegem. His shot was on target and well placed to the right, but Maier was onto it and tipped it way.

It was a sad way for Holland to go. Poor Cruyff and Neeskens didn't deserve this, but had again found an opponent they couldn't run over. Beckenbauer had been incredible, Matthäus an able deputy, and Müller had once again delivered at the death.

There was little between these two teams, except for different expectations forged from prior results. Germany's footballing success is proof that winning really is a habit, one that the Dutch have rarely caught.

Johan Cruyff

The most extraordinarily gifted player of the post-Pelé generation, Cruyff dragged Holland to the forefront of world football and was the embodiment of the "Total Football" that he did most to popularise.

He made his debut for Ajax at the age of 17 and was soon recognised as an immense talent. But Ajax were still a struggling side until Rinus Michels was appointed coach and helped mould Cruyff and Ajax into world-beaters.

Following a defeat by AC Milan in the 1969 European Cup Final, Ajax emerged as Europe's top team and won the first of three consecutive European Cups in 1971. The following year, Cruyff scored two goals and was the undoubted star as Ajax dominated Inter Milan. Another virtuoso display from Cruyff saw Ajax hold off Juventus in 1973, a match that turned out to mark the end of Ajax's run of dominance.

Europe's richest and most famous clubs had long eyed Cruyff. He resisted the urge until 1973 when - having been voted out as Ajax captain - Cruyff chose to follow Michels to Barcelona. The Spanish club won the league title in Cryuff's first season and the Dutch star was voted European Footballer of the Year for a record third time.

For all the great players that had come before him, there was something different about Cruyff. He roamed across the forward line, making goals and scoring them. His speed of foot was matched only by his quick mind and incredible dexterity.

When Holland arrived in West Germany for the 1974 World Cup, they weren't the favourites, but after some scintillating play in the early matches, few could see how they could be denied World Cup glory. With Cruyff to the fore, good teams like Argentina and Brazil were swept a side with a brand of high-speed attacking football not seen before.

The sky came tumbling down in the Final, however. With Cruyff well marked, Holland were unable to overcome West Germany.

Cruyff later became a highly successful and revolutionary coach with Ajax and Barcelona, where he introduced a new version of complete football.

Not always the most approachable figure off the field, the sight of Cruyff in full flow more than compensated.

Johan Cruyff: the ultimate "Total Footballer".

Lothar Matthäus

He didn't like to smile or head the ball, but there wasn't much else Matthäus didn't master in an astonishing 20-year international career.

Matthäus made his debut for West Germany in 1980, and played a bit-part role as his team progressed towards the European title. He had still not fully established himself as a regular two years later when West Germany lost in the World Cup Final, but did make his World Cup debut as a substitute against Chile. Eighteen years later, he played his 25th and final World Cup match in France - a clear record.

The finals in Mexico in 1986 marked Matthäus's coming of age. He announced himself as a world-class midfielder with several fine displays, including a goal against Morocco, before he took a man-marking assignment in the Final. Diego Maradona was such a threat that he warranted attention from the best, but West Germany hadn't learnt their lesson from 1966 where they used Franz Beckenbauer - their best midfielder - to mark Bobby Charlton. Matthäus kept Maradona relatively quiet, but Argentina won the game.

West Germany got their revenge four years later. With Matthäus now at his peak and joined by stars such as Andreas Brehme and Jürgen Klinsmann, the Germans rolled into the finals, although they needed penalties to dispose of a gutsy England. The rematch with Argentina was a shabby affair, the worst World Cup Final of all, but a Brehme penalty ensured glory to West Germany. In the earlier matches Matthäus had looked unstoppable, especially against Yugloslavia when he scored two marvellous goals.

He was named European Footballer of the Year and was widely considered the best player in the world. Quick, strong, with a powerful shot, firm tackle and playmaking skills to boot, he was the perfect modern midfielder. Only Johan Neeskens stands worthy of comparison.

After successful spells with Borussia Mönchengladbach and Bayern Munich, Matthäus moved to Inter Milan in Italy (along with Brehme and Klinsmann) and won the Uefa Cup in 1991.

Injury kept him out of the 1992 European Championships, and at 31 many expected that to be the end for Matthäus, but he had other ideas.

He returned to Bayern and, like Beckenbauer before him, switched to sweeper. Many doubted his ability to convert at such an advanced age, but four years later he was still there, a key factor in Bayern's run to Uefa Cup in 1996.

After missing the European Championships of 1996, Matthäus returned to the national side for his fifth World Cup in 1998 and rounded off an outstanding international record at the European Championships in 2000. In all, Matthäus won 150 caps and scored 23 goals. For once, the figures do justice to the legend.

GERMANY: *Sepp Maier; Berti Vogts (Karl-Heinz Schnellinger 88), Jürgen Kohler, Franz Beckenbauer, Andreas Brehme; Helmut Rahn (Jürgen Klinsmann 81), Lothar Matthäus, Fritz Walter (Willy Schulz 45), Wolfgang Overath; Karl-Heinz Rummenigge, Gerd Müller*
Subs not used: *Jürgen Croy, Bernd Schuster*
Goals: *Rahn 58, Müller 81*

HOLLAND: *Jan van Beveren; Wim Suurbier, Ronald Koeman, Barry Hulshoff (Frank de Boer 90), Ruud Krol; Frank Rijkaard, (Edgar Davids 82), Johan Neeskens, Wim van Hanegem; Ruud Gullit (Dennis Bergkamp 94) Marco van Basten, Johan Cruyff*
Subs not used: *Edwin van der Sar,, Rob Rensenbrink*
Goals: *Gullit 25, 71*

Penalties:

GERMANY; Müller scored, Beckenbauer scored, Matthäus scored, Klinsmann scored, Overath missed, Brehme scored

HOLLAND; Neeskens scored, Cruyff scored, Van Basten scored, Koeman scored, Bergkamp missed, Van Hanegem missed

Head-to-Head

Germany	Vs	Holland	Edge
Maier		Van Beveren	Germany
Vogts		Suurbier	Even
Brehme		Krol	Holland
Kohler		Hulshoff	Germany
Beckenbauer		Koeman	Germany
Rahn		Gullit	Holland
Matthäus		Neeskens	Even
Overath		Rijkaard	Even
Walter		Van Hanegem	Even
Rummenigge		Cruyff	Holland
Müller		Van Basten	Germany

Points: Germany 6 Holland 5

WEST GERMANY 2 HOLLAND 1

One of the most famous games of all-time, between two of the great teams. The clash between Holland and West Germany - between Cruyff and Beckenbauer, between poise and power - remains the most vivid football memory of the 1970s.

As the two sides advanced towards an inevitable showdown, Holland looked to have the edge.

Cruyff's team started with a handy 2-0 win against Uruguay and just kept on raising the bar, hammering Bulgaria and Argentina before ending Brazil's reign as World Champions. Only Sweden held out for a draw in a match that featured the most famous incarnation of Cryuff's turn.

West Germany struggled a little bit in the early stages, losing to their neighbours in the East, but slowly improved. Beckenbauer, who with his advances from the back gave his own interpretation of "Total Football", began to find his form and the Germans shifted into top gear at just the right time. Even so, Holland were most people's favourites before the Final in Munich.

Their confidence received a boost after just two minutes. Following a bewildering spell of possession football, Cruyff sped past Vogts and was brought down by Hoeness in the area. English referee Jack Taylor awarded the first World Cup Final penalty. Neeskens converted, giving Holland the perfect start.

For the next 20 minutes, the Dutch toyed with their opponents, passing rings around the Germans with football that was utterly sublime. But they failed to apply the killer blow. Some of the Dutch players said they were intent on humiliating the Germans, but it's doubtful that there was a conscious a plan.

After 24 minutes, Cruyff forged a chance for Rep who shot straight at Maier in the German goal. A moment later, West Germany were level. Hölzenbein moved in from the left and tumbled over as Jansen lunged in. There seemed to be minimal contact and Hölzenbein was known as one of the great German divers, but Taylor gave a penalty anyway. Breitner stepped up and brought his side level.

From a position of strength, Holland now looked in trouble. Vogts got to grips with Cruyff who drifted out of the game, and West Germany continued to attack. Vogts, Beckenbauer and Hoeness all came close, before the breakthrough finally arrived after 43 minutes.

The great Müller miss-controlled Bonhof's right-wing cross, pushing the ball away from goal. He then spun and shot past the static Jongbloed for the last of his 68 international goals.

In the second half Holland resumed their onslaught, but to no avail. Breitner cleared off the line and Maier made several fine saves - especially one block from a Neeskens blast.

Müller had a goal wrongly disallowed near the end for offside, but it didn't matter.

Twenty years after shocking Hungary, West Germany had again upset a favourite. Comparisons between the two games are obvious and Puskas's Hungary and Cruyff's Holland are the two best teams never to have won the World Cup. If there's a difference, however, it's that Holland lost to a magnificent side.

Some of the German players admitted that Holland were the better team; but Beckenbauer wasn't among them. "Had we played 10 games against Holland, we would certainly have won at least seven of them," he said.

Cruyff thought that playing on home soil gave West Germany an advantage. The venue certainly had something to do with it, but so did Beckenbauer, Maier and Müller.

Third-Place Play-off

ITALY 2 HOLLAND 1

Had the semi-final draw matched Brazil with Holland, and Italy with Germany, these two teams might very well have met in the Final. It's hard to imagine that Brazil - who'd advanced by overcoming the best defences - would have withstood Holland's attack, while Italy have never had too much trouble with the Germans.

As it was, these great European powers had to settle for a place in the consolation final. The idea of deciding third-place seems pretty pointless, but the matches have historically proven relatively entertaining. Unfortunately, this match didn't follow the pattern. Holland rested some key players, including Cruyff, who had no interest in this sideshow. Italy also gave the reserves a run-out, and after their brave display against Brazil reverted to their defensive roots.

Rensenbrink, starting on the left, crafted the first chance, running past Burgnich before pulling it back for Neeskens to shoot high and wide.

Italy then struck twice in three minutes - effectively killing the game. After a Dutch move broke down, Mazzola fed Riva who cantered up field and timed his release to Piola perfectly. The big striker slotted home with ease. Tardelli - a strong presence on the right throughout the competition - made a forceful run down the flank and provided a measured but bobbling cross. Rivera was on to it and guided his shot past Van Beveren to make it 2-0.

For the next hour Holland retained most of the possession but created precious few openings. Bergkamp and Koeman both missed chances and Gullit hit the post after powering past Facchetti on the right. The introduction of Van Hanegem gave Holland some hope. His strong run set Van Basten free to score his fifth goal of competition, but he didn't seem overly delighted.

Neeskens and Tardelli clashed in a violent 50-50 near the end - no game would be a tackle-free zone with them about.

When the final whistle blew, Italy had secured third-place, but it remained a case of what might have been.

ITALY: *Gianpiero Combi; Tarcisco Burgnich, Gaetano Scirea, Ricardo Ferri, Giacinto Facchetti; Marco Tardelli, Romeo Benetti, Gianni Rivera (Roberto Baggio 79), Sandro Mazzola; Silvio Piola, Luigi Riva (Paolo Rossi 55)*
Subs not used: *Dino Zoff, Giuseppe Meazza, Paolo Maldini*
Goals: *Piola 15, Rivera 17*

HOLLAND: *Jan van Beveren; Wim Suurbier, Ronald Koeman (Frank de Boer 45), Barrie Hulshoff, Ruud Krol; Frank Rijkaard, (Wim Jansen 45), Johan Neeskens, Dennis Bergkamp (Wim Van Hanegem 61); Ruud Gullit, Marco van Basten, Rob Rensenbrink*
Subs not used: *Edwin van der Sar, Marc Overmars*
Goal: *Van Basten 79*

Final

BRAZIL 2 WEST GERMANY 1

Between them they've participated in all but one of the post-war Finals, but not once have Brazil and (West) Germany met in the World Cup. In their very separate ways, these two teams have dominated modern football.

So far in this tournament Brazil had been the more impressive. The individual skills of Pelé, Ademir and Garrincha had been the highlight, but they'd gelled as a team as well. Indeed, the six goals conceded by Brazil was one less than by Germany, supposedly the ultimate bastion of organisation and discipline.

Both teams were unchanged from the semi-finals and both line-ups were full of experience. For Germany, only Rummenigge had not won a World Cup, and he'd been in two Finals. Brazil had nine players with a winner's medal, plus Ademir who deserved one.

Didi looked the most comfortable in the early stages. Without a man-marker he took advantage, roaming across the pitch and dictating the pace of the game. Matthäus eventually latched on to him, but not before Brazil had scored the opening goal. From Didi's long pass, Pelé cantered down the right and was brought down by Vogts as he cut inside. Didi took the free kick himself. Maier did well to touch it onto the bar, but Pelé squeezed in front of Kohler to score from the rebound.

The Germans have twice come from behind to win in World Cup Finals and so retained their composure.

Walter had been disappointing in the tournament so far and was lucky to have started ahead of Schuster. But the intelligent playmaker finally imposed himself and began to find recipients for his accurate passes. Brehme, who'd warmed up for Garrincha with Matthews and Gullit, was picked out on the left. Rummenigge connected with his curling cross, but Gilmar saved comfortably. Walter was soon back in possession and fed Rahn on the right. His first-time ball across the area was tailor-made for Müller, but he inexplicably miscued from five yards. Finally, Walter's wiles produced a goal. Matthäus ran onto a probing through ball and hit a strong right-footed shot onto the far post. Müller was on to it and tapped home.

164

THE MATCHES

The two teams traded chances until mid-way through the second half. Pelé lobbed over the bar, Walter drew a good save from Gilmar, and Garrincha beat Brehme and put in a dangerous cross that Kohler did well to clear.

It was Garrincha who created the next goal. He received the ball from Didi and ran at the heart of Germany's defence. As the white shirts amassed around him he knocked out a pass to Carlos Alberto. The adventurous right-back put a low, high-speed ball across the area. Vogts raised his foot to clear it, but Pelé head reached it first. Maier dived, but only after the ball was over the line. It was a brave move from Brazil's legendary number ten - in the 1960s or 1970s a defender in Vogts's position might have followed through with his kick. But, for all his toughness, Vogts wasn't really built that way, and if anyone deserved reverence it was Pelé. Having been kicked out of two World Cups he was enjoying this encore.

Germany weren't prepared to surrender just yet. Beckenbauer moved forward and shot narrowly wide, and Overath swung a free kick over the bar, but it wasn't supposed to be this time. Just before the end, Müller swivelled on a Schuster pass and shot hard and low. Gilmar was beaten but Djalma Santos cleared off the line.

It was finally over. After 32 matches, Brazil were crowned the world's greatest footballing power.

Germany had put up a good fight, but were up against the weight of history. More often that not, the World Cup has been won by the team with the tournament's best player - some things never change.

BRAZIL: *Gilmar; Carlos Alberto, Júlio César, Djalma Santos, Nílton Santos; Dunga, Didi; Garrincha, Ademir (Gérson 81), Pelé, Roberto Rivelino (Mário Zagallo 75)*
Subs not used: *Claudio Taffarel, Edinho, Romario*
Goals: *Pelé 20, 66*

GERMANY: *Sepp Maier; Berti Vogts, Jürgen Kohler, Franz Beckenbauer, Andreas Brehme (Karl-Heinz Schnellinger 80); Helmut Rahn, Lothar Matthäus, Fritz Walter, Wolfgang Overath (Bernd Schuster 74); Karl-Heinz Rummenigge (Jürgen Klinsmann 77), Gerd Müller*
Subs not used: *Jürgen Croy, Willy Schulz*
Goal: *Müller 35*

Head-to-Head

Brazil	Vs	Germany	Edge
Gilmar		Maier	Germany
Carlos Alberto		Vogts	Brazil
Nílton Santos		Brehme	Brazil
Júlio César		Beckenbauer	Germany
Djalma Santos		Kohler	Even
Garrincha		Rahn	Brazil
Dunga		Matthäus	Germany
Didi		Walter	Brazil
Rivelino		Overath	Even
Pelé		Rummenigge	Brazil
Ademir		Müller	Germany

Points: Brazil 6 Germany 5

Pelé

He is the standard by which all great players are measured, the most famous figure in sport and the greatest footballer of all-time. Pelé doesn't know where his nickname came from, but today every fan is well aware of what the name stands for; it means footballing perfection.

He arrived on the world scene as a 17-year old prodigy and signed off 12 years later with a series of astonishing performances that confirmed his status as a demi-god.

He made his debut for Santos in 1956 and played his first game for Brazil a year later. He still wasn't a regular when he arrived in Sweden for his first World Cup, but after a mixed start, the team's senior players pushed for his inclusion. After displaying his skills against the Soviet Union, he scored the only goal to defeat Wales, notched up a hat-trick against France in the semi-final, and another two in the Final.

Six goals in four matches was impressive, but it was the completeness of Pelé's game that set him apart. There'd been skilled players before - and perhaps the likes of Puskas were even as gifted as Pelé. But the Hungarian and the other 50s entertainers were from a different time.

In the 1960s, speed, strength and tactical awareness became as important as individual talent. Pelé was the first player able to combine the ball skills of his predecessors with the physical and mental attributes required in the modern game.

By the time Brazil travelled to Chile to defend the World Cup in 1962, Pelé was firmly established as football's top man. In the first game against Mexico he confirmed his status with a remarkable individual goal, but Pelé was carrying an injury and, in the next match, his groin finally gave way. Brazil retained the World Cup, but their victory will never be remembered in the same way as 1958 because something - the main thing - was missing.

Before things got better, they got worse. In his third World Cup in 1966, Pelé was under tremendous pressure. Much to his own dismay Brazil had not brought in many new players and the side was in decline. His country's fortunes rested with him, and the opposition knew it. First Bulgaria, and then Portugal, hacked at the great man until vicious Portugese defender Morais left Pelé needing help to leave the pitch.

He talked about avoiding future World Cups, but fortunately he was persuaded to take a final bow on the big stage. In Mexico 1970, Pelé took the game to new levels. He scored four times in the competition, but it's three goals he didn't score that left the greatest impression. The header that drew the best from Banks showed the Brazilian's tremendous athleticism, while near misses against Czechoslovakia and Uruguay demonstrated an imagination second to none. Against the Czechs he produced a lob from half way that floated just wide, and he beat Uruguay's goalkeeper without even touching the ball. Running on to a through ball he went one way, while the ball went the other. It didn't go in, but who cared? In the Final he headed in the opening goal and then supplied the perfect pass to Carlos Alberto who converted the so-called "President's Goal".

Pelé ended his international career a year later after 77 goals in 91 full caps. He was only 30 and could have played on, but he'd done enough.

He ended his career with the New York Cosmos and helped bring some credibility to "soccer" in the USA. Throughout it all, Pelé remained a wonderful ambassador for the game, a rare example of unflawed genius.

RESULTS

Quarter-finals

Brazil	3-1	Uruguay
Germany	2-1aet	England
Italy	3-2aet	Argentina
Holland	2-1	France

Semi-finals

Brazil	3-2	Italy
Germany	2-2	Holland (5-4 on pens)

Third-place play-off

Italy	1-0	Holland

Final

BRAZIL	**2-1**	**GERMANY**

Leading Goal Scorers

Player	Country	Goals
Gerd Müller	Germany	8
Pelé	Brazil	6
Johan Cruyff	Holland	5
Eusebio	Portugal	5
Ademir	Brazil	5
Marco van Basten	Holland	5
Just Fontaine	France	4
Alfredo Di Stefano	Argentina	3
Gabriel Batistuta	Argentina	3
Gunnar Nordahl	Sweden	3

WHAT MIGHT HAVE BEEN...

When the iron curtain fell in the early 1990s the football world was greatly impacted. Suddenly, a plethora of newly independent countries entered the scene. But as Croatia, Russia and Slovakia made their bows, we had to say goodbye to some established football powers. The Soviet Union, Czechoslovakia and Yugoslavia all made their impact at the World Cup. Czechoslovakia, for example, twice made the Final, while between them Yugoslavia and Croatia have three times made the semi-finals. Had they stayed intact, all three former-countries would have qualified for the finals.

SOVIET UNION

Russia made the finals, but could only have done better had they been able to draw on the best of the rest. Ukraine produced many fine players in the 1980s, especially in defence, which was not Russia's strong suit. Georgia's fine defenders Aleksandr Chivadze, Revaz Dzodzuashvili and Murtaz Khurtsilava, and Nikita Simonian, the greatest player from Armenia, just missed out.

Lev Yashin; Vladimir Besonov, Oleg Kuznetsov, Albert Schesternev, Anatoly Demianenko; Valery Voronin, Igor Netto, Vasily Rats; Igor Chislenko, Eduard Streltsov, Oleg Blokhin

CZECHOSLOVAKIA

Although the Czech Republic has faired the better since the dissolution, many of the great Czechoslovak teams were built around Slovak players. The combined all-time team blends strong defence and skilled midfielders. The forwards aren't bad either.

Frantisek Plánicka; Karol Dobias, Antos Ondrus, Jan Popluhar, Ladislav Novák; Josef Masopust, Antonin Panenka, Pavel Nedved; Marian Masny, Oldrich Nejedly, Zdénék Nehoda

YUGOSLAVIA

Since the very first World Cup, Yugoslavia has continued to produce world-class players. Croatia, the new Yugoslavia, and Bosnia all have strong all-time teams. Together, the line-up is especially pleasing. Slovenian Srecko Katanec and Bosnian Ivica Osim were closest to breaking the stranglehold of Serbian and Croatian players.

Vladimir Beara; Ivan Buljan, Josip Katalinski, Velimir Zajec, Fahrudin Jusufi; Dragan Stojkovic, Ivan Gudelj, Dragoslav Sekularac, Dragan Dzajic; Davor Suker, Stjepan Bobek

ALL-TIME GREATEST 100 PLAYERS

Rank	Player	Position	Country
1	Pelé	Inside-forward (Striker)	Brazil
2	Diego Maradona	Left/Centre Midfielder/Striker	Argentina
3	Alfredo Di Stéfano	Centre-forward (Centre-midfielder)	Argentina/Spain/Columbia
4	Franz Beckenbauer	Wing-half (Centre-midfielder)/ Sweeper	WestGermany (Germany)
5	Johan Cruyff	Centre-midfielder/Left-wing/Striker	Holland
6	Ferenc Puskas	Inside Left (Striker)	Hungary
7	George Best	Left/Right-wing	Northern Ireland
8	Garrincha	Right-wing	Brazil
9	Michel Platini	Centre-midfielder	France
10	Bobby Charlton	Left-wing/Centre-midfielder/Striker	England
11	Lev Yashin	Goalkeeper	Russia
12	Gerd Müller	Striker	West Germany (Germany)
13	Eusébio	Striker	Portugal
14	Juan Schiaffino	Inside-Left (Centre-midfielder/Striker)	Uruguay/Italy
15	Bobby Moore	Centre-back	England
16	Didi	Inside-Forward (Centre-midfielder)	Brazil
17	Johan Neeskens	Centre-midfielder	Holland
18	Lothar Matthäus	Centre-midfielder	WestGermany/Germany
19	Franco Baresi	Sweeper/Centre-back	Italy
20	Luis Monti	Centre-half (Centre-midfielder)	Argentina/Italy
21	Obdulio Varela	Centre-half (Centre-back/midfielder)	Uruguay
22	Zinedine Zidane	Centre-midfielder	France
23	Stanley Matthews	Right-wing	England
24	Paolo Maldini	Left-back	Italy
25	Giuseppe Meazza	Inside/Centre-forward/Centre-midfielder	Italy
26	Marco van Basten	Striker	Holland
27	Daniel Passarella	Centre-back/Sweeper	Argentina
28	Ruud Gullit	Right-wing/Striker/Centre-midfielder	Holland
29	Carlos Alberto	Right-back	Brazil
30	José Leandro Andrade	Right-half (Centre-midfielder/Right-back)	Uruguay
31	Denis Law	Striker	Scotland
32	Matthias Sindelar	Centre-forward (Centre-midfielder/Striker)	Austria
33	José Nasazzi	Right-back (Centre-back/Sweeper)	Uruguay
34	Marcel Desailly	Centre-back/Centre-midfielder	France
35	Ademir	Inside Forward (Striker)	Brazil
36	Nílton Santos	Left-back	Brazil
37	Gordon Banks	Goalkeeper	England
38	Gérson	Inside Forward (Centre-midfielder)	Brazil
39	Zico	Striker/Centre-midfielder	Brazil
40	Ernst Ocwirk	Centre-half (Centre-midfielder)	Austria
41	Helmut Rahn	Right-wing	West Germany (Germany)
42	Silvio Piola	Centre-forward (Striker)	Italy
43	Romário	Striker	Brazil
44	Giacinto Facchetti	Left-back	Italy
45	Karl-Heinz Rummenigge	Striker/Right-wing	West Germany (Germany)
46	Dino Zoff	Goalkeeper	Italy
47	Kazimierz Deyna	Centre-midfielder	Poland
48	Gheorghe Hagi	Centre-midfielder	Romania
49	Francisco Gento	Left-wing	Spain
50	Albert Shesternev	Centre-back/Sweeper	Russia (Soviet Union)

51	Sándor Kocsis	Inside-Right (Striker)	Hungary
52	Günnar Nordahl	Centre-forward (Striker)	Sweden
53	Ricardo Zamora	Goalkeeper	Spain
54	Raymond Kopa	Inside-forward (Centre-midfielder/Right-wing	France
55	Roberto Baggio	Striker	Italy
56	Rivaldo	Centre-midfielder	Brazil
57	Germano	Centre-back	Portugal
58	József Bozsik	Right-half (Centre-midfielder)	Hungary
59	Luis Figo	Right-wing/Centre-midfielder	Portugal
60	Frank Rijkaard	Centre-midfielder/Centre-back	Holland
61	Jürgen Klinsmann	Striker	West Germany/Germany
62	Mario Kempes	Striker	Argentina
63	Ronaldo	Striker	Brazil
64	Luis Suárez	Inside-Forward (Centre-midfielder)	Spain
65	Roberto Rivelino	Left-wing/Centre-midfielder	Brazil
66	Mário Zagallo	Left-wing	Brazil
67	Kenny Dalglish	Striker	Scotland
68	Dragoslav Sekularac	Inside-Right (Centre-midfielder)	Yugoslavia
69	Mário Coluna	Inside-Right (Centre-midfielder)	Portugal
70	Wolfgang Overath	Inside-Left (Centre-midfielder)	West Germany (Germany)
71	Ruud Krol	Left-back/Sweeper	Holland
72	Fritz Walter	Inside-Right (Centre-midfielder)	West Germany (Germany)
73	Frantisek Plánicka	Goalkeeper	Czech Republic (Czechs)
74	Silvio Marzolini	Left-back	Argentina
75	Gianni Rivera	Centre-midfielder	Italy
76	Elias Figueroa	Centre-back	Chile
77	Flórián Albert	Centre-forward (Centre-midfielder/Striker)	Hungary
78	Kurt Hamrin	Right-wing	Sweden
79	Josef Masopust	Left-half (Centre-midfielder)	Czech Republic (Czechs)
80	Héctor Scarone	Inside-Forward (Striker/Centre-midfielder)	Uruguay
81	Oldrich Nejedly	Centre-forward (Centre-midfielder/Striker)	Czech Republic (Czechs)
82	Gabriel Batistuta	Striker	Argentina
83	Grzegorz Lato	Right-wing	Poland
84	Wim van Hanegem	Centre-midfielder	Holland
85	Teófilo Cubillas	Inside-Forward (Centre-midfielder/Striker)	Peru
86	Marco Tardelli	Centre/Right Midfielder	Italy
87	Duncan Edwards	Left-half (Centre-midfielder/Centre-back)	England
88	Alex James	Inside-Forward (Centre midfielder)	Scotland
89	Uwe Seeler	Striker/Centre-midfielder	West Germany (Germany)
90	Jairzinho	Right-wing/Inside Forward (Striker)	Brazil
91	Dragan Dzajic	Left-wing	Yugoslavia
92	Gary Lineker	Striker	England
93	Paul van Himst	Inside-Forward (Striker/Centre-midfielder)	Belgium
94	Zoltán Czibor	Left-wing	Hungary
95	Just Fontaine	Centre-forward (Striker)	France
96	Gaetano Scirea	Centre-back/Sweeper	Italy
97	Victor Rodríguez Andrade	Right-half (Right-back)	Uruguay
98	John Charles	Centre-forward/half (Striker/Centre-back)	Wales
99	Roy Keane	Centre-midfielder	Republic of Ireland
100	Bernd Schuster	Centre-midfielder	West Germany (Germany)

THE ALL-TIME XI

Any book of this type wouldn't be complete without an All-Time selection. Again I've tried to retain a reasonable structure, with four defenders, a ball winner and an out-and-out goal scorer. There's a log-jam of left-sided players at the top of the 100, but the likes of Cruyff and Pelé are versatile enough to get by.

First Team

Lev Yashin; Carlos Alberto, Bobby Moore, Franz Beckenbauer, Paolo Madini; Johan Cruyff, Johan Neeskens, Alfredo Di Stefano, Diego Maradona; Pelé, Ferenc Puskas

Second Team

Gordon Banks; Victor Rodríguez Andrade, Franco Baresi, Obdulio Varela, Nílton Santos; Garrincha, Lothar Matthäus, Michel Platini, George Best; Gerd Muller, Bobby Charlton

BIBLIOGRAPHY

Cantor, Andrés, *Goooal! A Celebration of Soccer*
Fireside, New York, 1996
The Daily Telegraph, Century of Sport, edited by Welch, David
MacMillan, London, 1998
Downing David, *The Best of Enemies: England v Germany,*
A Century of Football Rivalry
Bloomsbury, London, 2000
Faber Book of Soccer, edited by Ian Hamilton,
Faber and Faber, London, 1992
Freddi, Chris, *The Complete Book of the World Cup*
Collins Willow, London, 1998
Freddi, Chris, *England Football Fact Book*
Guinness, Enfield, Middlesex, 1996
Gardner, Paul, *The Simplest Game: The Intelligent Fan's*
Guide to the World of Soccer
Macmillan, New York, 1996
Glanville, Brian, *The Story of the World Cup*
Faber and Faber, London, 2001
The Guinness Book of Football, edited by Benato, Max
Guinness, London, 2000
Hansen, Alan with Haylett, Trevor, *Six of the Best*
Hodder & Stoughton, London, 1991
Leatherdale, Clive, *England: The Quest for the World Cup,*
A Complete Record
Two Heads Publishing, Haywards Heath, West Sussex, 1994
Leatherdale, Clive, *Ireland: The Quest for the World Cup, A Complete Record*
Two Heads Publishing, Haywards Heath, West Sussex, 1994
Leatherdale, Clive, *Scotland: The Quest for the World Cup,*
A Complete Record
Two Heads Publishing, Haywards Heath, West Sussex, 1994
Matthews, Peter with Buchanan, Ian and Mallon, Bill,
The Guinness International Who's Who of Sport
Enfield, Middlesex, 1993
Matthews, Peter & Buchanan, Ian, *All-Time Greats of British and Irish Sport*
Guinness, Enfield, Middlesex, 1995

174

Matthews, Stanley, *The Way it Was, My Autobiography*
Headline, London, 2000
Murray, Bill, *The World's Game: A History of Soccer*
University of Illinois, 1998
Nawrat, Chris & Hutchings, Steve, *The Sunday Times Illustrated
History of Football*
Ted Smart, London, 1994
Perfect Pitch: Home Ground, edited by Simon Kuper
Headline, London, 1997
Puskas on Puskas, edited by Taylor, Rogan and Jamrich, Klara
Robson Books, London, 1998
Radnedge, Keir, *The Complete Encyclopaedia of Scocer*
Carlton, London, 2000
Robinson, John, *Soccer: The European Championships*
Soccer Book Publishing, Cleethorpes, Lincs, 1996
Rollin, Glenda & Rollin, Jack, *Rothmans Football Year Book: 1999-2000*
Headline, London, 1999
Signy, Dennis & Giller, Norman, Golden Heroes:
Fifty Seasons of Footballer of the Year
Chameleon, London, 1997
The Sunday Times Sporting Century, edited by Alan English
Collins Willow, London, 1999
Tyrell, Tom & Meek, David, *The Hamlyn Illustrated History
of Manchester United*
Ted Smart, London, 1994
Wallachinsky, David, *The Complete Book of the Olympics*
Aurum Press, London, 2000
Winner, David, *Brilliant Orange*
Bloomsbury, London, 2000